Break Ground Without
Breaking Up

Break Ground Without Breaking Up

7 Keys to Securing a Strong Relationship
While Building or Remodeling Your Home

Sandy Berendes

Sandy Berendes
and
Laura Longville

Laura Longville

Mill City Press
Minneapolis, MN

Cheryl Weir and Associates
www.cherylweir.com
610-566-2543

www.buildremodelforcouples.com
www.breakgroundwithoutbreakingup.com

Mill City Press, Inc.
322 First Avenue N, 5th floor
Minneapolis, MN 55401
612.455.2293
www.millcitypublishing.com

ISBN-13: 978-1-63413-104-9
LCCN: 2014916912

Cover Design by Alan Pranke
Typeset by Sophie Chi

Printed in the United States of America

Advance Praise of *Break Ground Without Breaking Up*

"There's nothing like building a house to trigger a couple's emotional issues around money. Laura and Sandy offer valuable insights and practical tools to resolve those issues. This book is a great resource."

~Rick Kahler, MSFP,
CFP® and co-author of *Conscious Finance.*

"*Breaking Ground Without Breaking Up* is an essential read for any couple that is planning on building or remodeling. They have cracked the code of conflict that surrounds couples when they plan building projects. The book is empowering, educating and easy to read. It will save you money, heartache and time."

~Renee Rowe, LMSW, ACSW Director at Treeside
Institute for Clinical Advancement

"Having experienced just about everything possible in residential construction over the last 35 years, I have learned that each and every new home becomes a management experiment juggling the needs of many different people, from subs to owners and managing the chaos ultimately within a budget.

Sandy and Laura are successful at communicating the essential components of home construction projects while purposefully providing realistic solutions to reduce the stress and chaos of building or remodeling. Your project will become much easier and you will certainly maximize your opportunity for success by applying the concepts presented. Here's to your success!"

~Phil Olsen, President Olsen Real Estate ,
Olsen Development Company, Inc.

Dedication

This book is dedicated to couples that dream about building or remodeling their home. Home construction is an incredible experience and stressful on a relationship. Our hope is *Break Ground Without Breaking Up* will help keep the love in your relationship as you complete your project together.

Table of Contents

Part 1: Seven Keys

Key 1 / Make Sure the Timing is Right 1

1. Is the Timing Right for You and Your Family? 2

2. Is the Timing Right for the Real Estate Market? 3

3. Are You Ready to Grow in Your Relationship? 3

4. Do You Have the Right Tools? 4

5. Are You Ready to Get Help if You Need It? 7

6. Are You Ready to Have a Better Experience than Other Couples? 8

7. Reflection Questions 12

Key 2 / Dream Big 21

1. Two Dreamers, One Dream 22

2. What is the Style of Your Dream Home? 23

3. Mismatching Dreams 25

4. What to Do if You're in a Stalemate 27

5. Exercises 29

6. Reflection Questions 34

Key 3 / Let Your Needs and Values be Your Guide

1. It's Easy to Get Lost in a Project   37

2. Your Needs and Values   40

3. No Right or Wrong   45

4. Reflection Questions and Activities   50

Key 4 / Plan Sensibly

1. The "B" Word   54

2. Opposites Attract   58

3. What Are Your Money Beliefs?   63

4. How to Develop a Budget   64

5. Exercises and Recommended Resource   66

Key 5 / Live in Financial Integrity

1. Financial Infidelity   70

2. The Danger of Secrets   71

3. The S.A.F.E. Way to Deal with Money   74

4. We Don't Really Own Anything   79

5. Reflection Questions and Recommended Resource   83

Key 6 / Expect the Unexpected

1. Detours   85

2. Unexpected Building Disasters   89

3. Losses Prior to the Beginning of the Build   91

4. Life Trauma During the Build   94

5. Unexpected Good News   95

6. How We Deal with the Unexpected
   Will Make the Difference   99

7. Reflection Questions   101

Key 7 / Survive the Stress

1. Focus on What You Can Control   106

2. Change Your Thinking   106

3. Change Your Attitude   107

4. Take a Break   108

5. Communicate in a Positive Way   109

6. 7 Simple Ways to Strengthen Your
   Relationships   113

7. Reflection Questions   116

Part 2: Tools of the Trade

▶ Quick Reference Checklist   120

▶ How to Hire a General Contractor   121

   ▪ Questions to Ask a General Contractor   121

   ▪ What a General Contractor Wants
     You to Know   124

▶ How to Hire an Interior Designer   132

   ■ Questions to Ask an Interior Designer   134

   ■ What an Interior Designer Wants
You to Know   135

▶ How to Hire a Therapist or Life Coach

   ■ Questions to Ask a Therapist or Life Coach   136

     ○ What a Therapist or Life Coach
Wants You to Know   137

▶ Resources

   ■ Therapy/Coaching   141

   ■ Interior Design   141

   ■ Home Design   141

   ■ Finances   142

▶ Celebrate   145

Create Your Own Key Ring

● Personal Summary of Each Key   150

● Contact Information of Your Key Team Players   154

● Conclusion   155

● Home Prayer   155

Appendix A: Dream Big, Real Big Diagram 2   157

Appendix B: Needs and Values Questionnaire   159

Acknowledgments

I (LAURA) WANT TO THANK SANDY FOR INVITING ME to write this book with her. I am grateful to Sandy for believing in me, my skills as a therapist and for hanging together throughout this adventure. Without her dream and vision of helping couples sustain their love under home construction; this book would not be in your hands. Sandy's creative ability to capture the essence and uniqueness of each home and family is admired.

Mark Longville, my husband, friend and co-builder of our dream home, thank you from the bottom of my heart for your passion for our home and encouraging me to write about what I know. To my girls, Taylor, Sawyer and Carter: love you and thanks for the memories we create in our amazing home.

Our new home would not be possible without Phil Olsen, our builder and my Uncle. He caught the vision of what we wanted in our new home, designed it and made it a reality. Thanks for guiding us through the custom home building process, caring for the project like it was your own, sticking with us through a "few" stressful situations and keeping our family bond in the forefront of all we did.

We want to thank God for all he has given us and for his direction throughout our project. With gratitude we thank Carmen Berry, our book writing coach as she was vital to helping our book-writing dream become a reality.

Thanks to the many couples I (Sandy) have had the privilege to counsel with over the years. You give me courage to muck through the complications in life; the inspiration to keep going and hope that hard work, dedication and commitment build strong relationships.

Although they could not know, my clients have inspired me to write this book. The stories I have in this book are a result of the transparency of very special clients that I will never forget. I acknowledge them for entrusting me with their words and their dreams of creating their sacred spaces, their homes. They have enriched my life with a lot more than money.

I acknowledge my co-author, Laura Longville. She has been an angel to me in a lot more ways than just writing this book with me. Our paths kept crossing in "coincidental" ways for a long time before she agreed to write a book with the likes of me. You just know when someone in your life is led to you by God.

I acknowledge general contractor, Andy Scull, (gc1) President of Scull Construction in Rapid City, S.D, for his honesty and forthright answers as I interviewed him about hiring and interviewing a general contractor. I am proud to say he is also my son.

My daughter and son-in-law, Ami and Nate Larson, have been a huge source of support for me. Not everyone has been able to catch my vision about writing a book like this. They have and I appreciate them for listening to me and not throwing a wet blanket on my dream of helping couples with the stress of blending their dreams through the process of building a home together. I want to acknowledge Ami and Nate for being the "Ami and Nate" in this book. I asked them many times if they wanted to change their names to protect their privacy. Each time they declined that protection because they have taken a light-hearted approach now that the remodel is history. Transparency is natural for them.

I want to acknowledge that" Inner Voice" inside me that nagged me to death to get started writing. I was promised that my co-writing angel would appear. She did. Laura and I have learned a whole new world together as we put one foot in front of the other to bring this book to fruition. Writing a book is a learning experience like I've never had before. "A Course in Miracles"," Volume Three", a "Manual for Teachers", states, "When the student is ready, the teacher appears." Ready or not, here is our book. It is intended to be of service to you.

Let's Get Started!

WE WROTE THIS BOOK TO GIVE YOU A relational floor plan, and a set of keys to help you navigate the journey of home construction with as little stress and conflict as possible. We are Sandy, a skilled interior designer, and Laura, an experienced therapist, both of whom have traveled this often difficult path with couples engaged in-home construction.

Through the years, Sandy has experienced the reality of working with couples where tension, fear and anxiety control the home building or remodeling process. Laura has heard horror stories of people who, while building their home, experienced extreme strife, unhappiness and sometimes divorce.

Sandy impressively assisted Laura in updating her office space years ago. Laura knew when it came time to build her dream home, Sandy was the right person to help her and her husband avoid the relationship pitfalls. Sandy not only guided Laura and Mark through the construction process, but also helped them communicate their dreams with each other, and come out of the process a stronger, more devoted couple.

Shortly after putting the finishing touches on Laura's home, Sandy and Laura discovered that combining their professional expertise with their personal experiences was the perfect foundation for a much-needed relationship guide for building couples.

The most significant truth we've discovered is that *a couple's relationship will be remodeled along with their home*. Couples we have worked with illustrate that accepting and working with this reality radically decreases the stress, and results in more mutual satisfaction throughout the home construction process. A blueprint is as vital to building a home as a relational blueprint is to maintaining a stable partnership.

You may notice we include couples of all definitions and refer to you as "significant other" or "spouses". We don't assume you are married but are committed to each other and dedicated to building your lives together. Therefore, we refer to your commitment as a "relationship." "coupleship" or "marriage."

Break Ground without Breaking Up is full of solutions, ideas and resources to help you productively reach two significant goals. First to build your dream home or remodel your castle to be its best and, second, to keep the love in your relationship! In each chapter you will find reflections, questions or activities you can apply to your personal life.

Our professions have provided us with many first hand stories and real life examples directly applicable to this issue. The names and some identifying information have been changed to protect the privacy and dignity of our clients. You may find yourself in these stories, experience relief, and feel encouraged and hopeful.

In addition, we present a variety of designer tips and relationship tools you can use, such as the art of celebration used by one couple we worked with named Carrie and John. They learned early in their relationship to keep things light — not to take life so seriously, to celebrate the simple things in life. During their building project, each Friday they brought pizza and beer for the workers as they looked over the progress they made throughout the week. This was a very simple activity that helped them focus on the positive each week, even when there were setbacks. Being prepared and equipped for a home construction project will assure your relationship will be enhanced, not weakened, by this significant joint-venture.

How to Get the Most From This Book

The information in this book will be most helpful to read prior to breaking ground. However, it is never too late to gain insight and apply proven tips to both your marriage and your home upgrade. We are going to walk you through a process, starting with envisioning your dream home to actually walking through the front door. We have divided the book into seven steps, one for each key to unlock your new dream home—and upgraded relationship. It is important you read this book from beginning to end, taking each key in order.

Each key builds upon another, as you can see from the following preview.

Key 1: Make Sure the Time is Right

Building or remodeling a home is a major life event, one that will change your family, and most certainly your relationship, forever. The success of your journey as a couple and a family will depend on how intentional you are about the decisions you make. No one can predict the future, but taking time to assess whether the timing is right for a project of this magnitude is crucial. We outline six significant issues to help you discern if now is the best time, or if this endeavor will be more successful at a later date.

Key 2: Dream Big

Dreaming is a significant part of the overall process. You will be encouraged to dream big and unearth the elements you desire in your new home. After creating a list of your needs and "must-haves," you will bring your dream into the realm of what is possible for you as a couple.

Unless you have an unlimited budget (and few do) some of the dreams you and your partner have may not be realized. Identifying which things you can afford and what needs to be eliminated from your plan, or at least postponed for this project, will help both of you to avoid serious disappointments and possible conflict.

Key 3: Let Your Needs and Values Be Your Guide

Having a personal guidance system akin to a map or GPS will keep you directed and focused, and help you make decisions aligned with your values and goals. The Needs and Values questionnaire will not only assist you in building or remodeling your home but also in strengthening your relationship.

Key 4: Plan Sensibly

Your money, beliefs and style influence your relationship and building project. This chapter will help you review your budget to see if it reflects your values, needs and goals to guide your home building or remodeling decisions. Reflection questions are mixed throughout this chapter to help you become financially conscious and prepared.

Key 5: Live in Financial Integrity

Your home construction budget will help you control your costs. Maintaining financial integrity is the key to sustaining honor, stability and strength in your relationship throughout your remodel or building. There is a SAFE way to keep your eyes on the goals and love in your relationship. Be ready to be deeply challenged in this chapter.

Key 6: Expect the Unexpected

The timing of the building project is important. The project is time consuming and requires a significant amount of your attention. Even when a project is initiated at a time when you're free to devote what is needed, life can intrude on our plans. This chapter will help you learn to move through unexpected life events, such as death and grief, injuries, and even some "nice" surprises. The reflection questions will help you apply the information to your own circumstances.

Key 7: Survive the Stress

This chapter helps couples identify when stress is running, and ruining, the project, what to do if you get stuck and how to apply communication tools to move forward. Adding those finishing touches, celebrating your successes and documenting your process will preserve a positive experience to you. Reflection questions and activities will help you apply the lessons.

PART 2
Tools of the Trade

Having the right tools, resources and perfect team players is necessary for your construction endeavor! Here we offer advice from general contractors on what's important for you to know prior to starting your project. Also contained within this section is expert counsel on hiring the interior designer and guidance on finding the suitable therapist or life coach to add to your team. Celebration suggestions round out this chapter that hopefully inspire you to commemorate your venture.

Create Your Own Key Chain

Knowing which key to use to open your front door is crucial to entering your new home! In the same way, knowing when to use all the keys on the key ring is vital to a successful relationship. This chapter explains how to use the keys at the proper time. We also have included various resources to foster the love in your relationship during the course of your construction activities.

We want to help you preserve and protect your relationship while your home is under construction. The seven keys we share will help you to co-create a clear plan of action, to enjoy your relationship throughout the construction process and to celebrate your progress.

We can't say this enough: take the time to prepare. Do as much preparation ahead of time as possible. You will be rewarded! You'll have a sense of peace from knowing you've done all you can do to maximize the success of your venture. That doesn't mean there won't be unexpected things happening. Because there will be. What it does mean is that your remodel or home building project will reflect you. You will be happy, you'll be pleased with what you have and your relationship will thrive.

Before they knew it, Nathan and Ami were fighting about granite countertops, how many outlets to put in each room and how much this project was going to cost them. Only married for eleven months, the discord was hard on their dreams for a long future.

～～

"Sure hope you don't get a divorce if you build that house," Andy had said to his brother, Don. A year and a half year later, Don and his wife were filing for divorce and the home they'd built together had a "for sale" sign in the front yard.

～～

Annette told her home designer to give her two different invoices regarding furniture and window treatments. She said, "Please give me the accurate amount, and another I can give my husband that reflects a substantial amount less than the true costs. I can't stand all of the fighting, and if he knows the truth, he'll hit the roof!"

 ## Key One:

Make Sure the Timing is Right

RELATIONSHIPS CAN BE CHALLENGING AND complicated under the best of circumstances. But add the stress of constructing or remodeling a home and even the strongest relationships can be seriously tested. Couples that decide to build or re-model instead of buying an existing home are often motivated by the dream of making a functional, beautiful castle. They may share the vision of becoming the King and Queen of their estate. But without realizing it, the King may have a mental picture of himself on the massive throne set in a medieval castle while the Queen sees herself living royally in a palace with modern amenities. Therein lies the issue of two people facing different goals in one relationship. The challenges begin, with many more to follow.

Before you launch your project, we want to ask you some very important questions. The answers will play a major part, not only in how well your house will turn out, but how strong your relationship will be at the end of this journey. We encourage you to work through these questions together as a couple, and to be as honest as you can with yourself and each other. At the end of this chapter are exercises built to help guide your decisions.

1. Is the Timing Right for You and Your Family?

One of the wisest men, King Solomon, pointed out the importance of timing when he said, "There is a right time for birth and for death, a right time to plant and to reap, a right time to kill and to heal, a right time to destroy and construct, a right time to laugh and to cry, a right time to lament and to cheer, a right time to make love and to abstain, a right time to embrace and to part, a right time to search and to let go, a right time to rip out and to mend, a right time to shut up and to speak up, a right time to love and to hate and a right time rage war and another to make peace."

We'd like to add that there's a right time to build or remodel a home.

However, having the wisdom to know when the time is right can be tricky. We want to help you look at, assess and determine ahead of time if re-modeling or building your home is right for you at this specific time. It's important to make an educated, conscious choice about the timing of your project.

You are wise to take the time to sort through your unique personal and family matters. After all, life is unpredictable. You are empowered when you make a conscious, well thought out choice rather than simply reacting to life's challenges.

2. Is the Timing Right for the Real Estate Market?

Another timing issue relates to the real estate market. This includes housing or land prices, mortgage interest rates, or economic issues. Investing in real estate can be a sound strategy when the prices and economy support it. In recent years, housing prices have dropped dramatically in many parts of the United States. Some predict prices will rebound. Others do not. In addition, interest rates drop and rise without predictability. It's important to know when to buy and when to sell.

Taking these changing trends into account will help you decide whether to sell your home and build a new one, or to keep your current home and remodel.

Real estate prices and lending aren't the only financial issues to consider. The current prices of construction materials, labor and building costs in your area are also important. A realistic review of the economic issues related to building or remodeling could save you a great deal of heart ache and financial loss, or set you on the path to following your dream.

"People grow through experience if they meet life honestly and courageously. This is how character is built."

~Eleanor Roosevelt

3. Are You Ready to Grow in Your Relationship?

One of the most significant issues to consider relates to your family relationships. Whatever strengths or weaknesses you have in your relationship prior to building or remodeling *will* reveal itself during the project. You and your spouse will make many decisions together in the coming months requiring you communicate clearly with each other. If you two make decisions honoring and respectful of each other you will continue to enjoy a strong relationship. Healthy, respectful communication is critical to success in a marriage *and* construction projects.

The opposite is true as well. The issues, challenges or problems in your relationship rise quickly to the surface in this situation. Alas, you won't be able to avoid them or stuff them away. Building or remodeling your home brings out the best and worst in your relationship.

We don't want to alarm you or scare you away from your goals. In fact, we want to show you how to use the home construction process to strengthen your relationship. To do that, it's important to realize that all relationships have strengths and weaknesses and they show up under pressure.

If you're not willing to grow, develop and mature in your relationship, we strongly encourage you to "pause and reflect" on why this is so. Reconsider if this is the time to start this project. There may be a better time to build or remodel. However, if you are willing to be self-analytical, then ask yourself to answer the next question.

4. Do You Have the Right Tools?

In the same way the right tools are imperative for successfully building a sound structure, you will need the proper intellectual, emotional and relational tools to cope with the stresses during the process. Our hope is your relationship will thrive so you can enjoy the home you build together.

As a couple, all your skills and assets will be needed. Building or remodeling your home is both a right and left brain endeavor. Your ability to envision your dream house, with both major and minor details, requires your creativity. On the other hand, it's important to engage your left brain's aptitude for organization and developing realistic plans. The book is full of checklists, problem solving, creative visualization and analytical activities to help integrate both sides of your brain.

In addition to the dreaming, thinking and strategic planning, you may find yourself physically engaged as well. Many Do It Yourselfers (DIY) do all or part of the building or remodeling themselves. Whether you participate to save money, or for the sheer satisfaction of seeing the fruit of your labor, it can be a physically demanding activity!

Building and remodeling also has a psychological aspect. Most homeowners are tied to their homes emotionally. Lady Antebellum, in their song, *Home is Where Your Heart Is*, inspires us to find "Home." You're not simply building a house; you are creating a home where you will live your life, along with family, friends and neighbors. The structure, the place where you live, is where your stories start and memories are created.

Perhaps one of the most important tools is the ability to handle surprises—and not the good kind of surprises. Even couples that scrupulously plan out every detail can find themselves faced with unanticipated, overwhelming problems. A great many things can hide inside walls, beneath the flooring or on the roof—poor electrical wiring, inadequate plumbing, molds, water damage and termites, to name just a few. In addition, your dream home may not match your city's zoning or health codes, which causes an abrupt halt to your building plans.

Financial concerns, physical exhaustion, multiple decisions to be made, and everyday life expectations may consume your daily thoughts. As we've said, construction has the tendency to bring out the worst in couples.

"If you're not willing to grow in your relationship, don't start your project."
~Laura Longville

As is true for any project, home builders, DIY'ers and remodelers rarely realize the full extent of how the process of construction alters their lives prior to starting a project. Let's face it. None of us fully know what we're getting into when we try something new. Some people may think, "We've got this under control. It won't be that hard. We'll be different!" And then they find out they face the same challenges as other couples.

Most couples aren't aware of how stressful the construction process is to relationships. Accept that you will run into difficulties. This will help you cope when they appear. It's easy to focus, dreamy-eyed, on a new home and ignore your relationship—that is, until you're fighting like cats and dogs. Understanding what to expect from start to completion is imperative so you don't fall prey to the same mistakes couples all over the country are facing.

Just like you need the right saws, devices and equipment to build your home, the same is true in your relationship. You need the right relationship tools to preserve and protect your relationship throughout your project.

5. Are You Ready to Get Help if You Need It?

You don't need to do your project by yourself! There are many people and resources available. You've picked up this book, which is a great first step (or even the tenth step).

In fact, not asking for help is the demise of many relationships, and sometimes the reason projects fail. It is important to have reliable and high quality professionals to complete your project. It's just as important to have good friends and supportive family.

Select a contractor with whom you can speak honestly, rely on, and trust. Take time to interview more than one contractor to make sure you are a good fit to work together. Get references and call them. It could save you money and heartache.

Other players on your team are your banker or mortgage person, CPA, financial advisor and insurance agent. Seek their advice and expertise. Add a therapist for your relationship struggles. It is amazing how an unbiased, objective third party who understands relationships can help your relationship.

Last, but not least, your friends and family can provide invaluable support. They share your excitement in your accomplishments and can support you through challenges. Give them an opportunity to work with you in achieving your dream house.

6. Are You Ready to Have a Better Experience than Other Couples?

We believe you will be better equipped than most couples simply because you've read this book. Your awareness of both the construction process and the demands placed on your relationship can prevent the horror stories many couples experience. If you know what to expect, you'll be better prepared to address the many decisions that need to be made in a cooperative way, rather than one that leads to unnecessary conflict.

Mike and Lisa are a good example of knowing their deeper need for remodeling along with the physical construction process. They had dreamt about remodeling their home for several years. When they bought their home, they had one child. When they were blessed with twin girls, becoming a family of five, they literally outgrew their home. All three kids were sleeping in the same crowded room. Lisa and Mike held different concerns about their limited home space.

Lisa viewed her home as a place for family and friends to get together. She wanted their home to be a shelter for their kids, friends and extended family, a gathering place.

Having organized, separate rooms for her kids to sleep in was significant for Lisa. When she was a child, her brothers and sisters all slept in the same room. It was messy and at times unsafe due to crammed furniture, clothing and children in one room. She was adamant it would be different for her children.

Paperclip Design Tip: Kids are people too. Allow them to pick paint colors and themes for their bedrooms. It can be their unique and playful space that reflects their growing personalities.

Mike had other concerns. For one, it was important for Mike to be debt free in eight to ten years. They had been saving for years in order to build an addition so they wouldn't have to add more debt. Mike was not willing to compromise on this goal. After much discussion and research, and taking both of their concerns into consideration, they decided to turn their garage into an additional bedroom and bathroom for the girls.

As is often the case, Mike and Lisa ran into unexpected problems. The builder discovered the current septic system could not handle the additional bathroom. This problem would cost them $5,000 more than they planned.

Unfortunately, Mike and Lisa hadn't planned for the unexpected. But they were able to talk at length about what to do, keeping in mind how important being debt free was to Mike and how critical it was for Lisa to have clean, separate bedrooms for her children. They tossed around the value of not taking on additional debt, not building the extra bathroom, selling one of their cars to help pay for the septic system, waiting to complete the project when they had more money, having Lisa get a part time job and lastly, not taking a vacation the next year. They were able to respectfully talk through what to do about the additional costs *and* honor each other's needs.

They decided to take the money they were going to use for vacation and put it toward the unexpected costs. Cooperation created a win-win solution. They created a way to pay for the unforeseen cost of a septic system.

Our hope is, like Lisa and Mike; your relationship will thrive through the process, rather than suffer, or even fall apart. As Stevie Wonder sings in his song *Overjoyed*, we believe you will be brought closer together and, soon, living in the home of your dreams. Remember, you're building the castle of your dreams or remodeling the palace you've imagined for years and it's important to you!

Overjoyed by Stevie Wonder:
"Over time, I've been building my castle of love
Just for two, though you never knew you were my reason
I've gone much too far, for you now to say
That I've got to throw my castle away.

Reflection Questions

These reflection questions will guide and direct you from a big picture perspective. Consider each question and rate your level of readiness. Determine what your strengths are and how to build upon them. You will notice areas that may need some extra help. That's OK. *Break Ground Without Breaking Up* can help strengthen and grow your relationship.

1. Is the timing right for us and our family?

Not Ready 1	2	3	4	5	6	7	8	9	Ready 10

- Are we, as a couple, able to communicate and make cooperative decisions at this point in our relationship?

- How will this impact our children? How does this affect our short term and long term financial goals?

- What are the outside events or situations that support (such as availability of new financial resources, solid support from extended family or friends, good health and energy levels) or discourage (such as job transition, medical issues, and extended family difficulties) undertaking building or remodeling at this time?

- Would there be a better time to do this? Maybe a year, or 5-10 years from now?

- Is the timing right for us and our family?

2. Is the Timing Right for the Real Estate Market?

Not Ready 1	2	3	4	5	6	7	8	9	Ready 10

- Are home prices increasing or decreasing? What does this mean for us and our family?

- Are interest rates increasing or decreasing? What does this mean for us and our family?

- What are the costs of construction materials, labor, building permits and other costs in our area?

- Is the timing right for the real estate market?

3. Are we ready to grow in our relationship?

Not Ready 1	2	3	4	5	6	7	8	9	Ready 10

- What are our strengths as a couple?

- What are our challenges as a couple?

- What can we do to strengthen our communication skills?

- Are we committed to listening to each other's needs with respect and coming up with a win-win solution?

- Are we ready to grow in our relationship?

4. Do we have the right tools?

No 1	2	3	Maybe 4	Maybe 5	Maybe 6	7	8	Yes 9	Yes 10

- How can we best utilize our creative talents and skills as a couple?

- How can we best utilize our organizational and planning skills as a couple?

- What does the word "home" mean to us, individually and as a couple?

- How well do we handle stress and uncertainty?

- Are we committed to being emotionally supportive of each other through the process?

- Do we have the right tools?

5. Are we ready to get help if we need it?

No 1	2	3	Maybe 4	Maybe 5	Maybe 6	7	8	Yes 9	Yes 10

- Family

- Friends

- Community networks

- Contractors

- Architects

- Skilled labor

- Therapist

- Other

6. Are we ready to have a better experience than other couples? Yes!

No 1	2	3	Maybe 4	Maybe 5	Maybe 6	7	8	Yes 9	Yes 10

- On a scale from one to ten: How open are we to new ideas?

- How will we utilize this book to help us during this process?

- In what other ways can we anticipate and prepare for this journey?

"A house is made of walls and beams, a home is built of love and dreams."

~Anonymous

 **Key Two:**

Dream Big

OWNING A HOME IS PART OF THE AMERICAN Dream. People plan, save and visualize about their dream home, sometimes for years. The American Heritage Dictionary defines a house as "a structure serving as a dwelling for one or more persons, especially for a family." It sits on a lot site of land, and usually has a lawn with some trees and plants. Inside there are rooms like a living room, kitchen, bedroom and bathrooms. All types and styles of homes will have these characteristics.

When you read the word "home" you probably have an idealized picture in your mind. A fond memory and warm emotions accompany those thoughts. A smile may come to your face as you remember that special Christmas or amazing childhood birthday party at your home. Do you remember walking into your home and smelling your favorite cookies or hearing the laughter of family members enjoying themselves?

As you can see, a house is so much more than mortar, lumber, windows, a roof and some furniture.

The walls, patio, kitchen and garage have much more meaning and value attached to them than the actual cost of the products to build them.

When you think of building or remodeling your house, your left brain most likely takes over. It's the part of your brain that is logical, uses critical thinking skills and incorporates language, reasoning and numbers.

When you say the word "home," often times you will have a right brain experience. Your right brain expresses and reads emotions, helps you be creative and intuitive.

The American Dream has more emotion attached to it than the numbers on the house designating the address. Whether you remodel or build—There's no place like home!

1. Two Dreamers, One Dream

Daydreaming is an essential precursor to launching your remodeling project or taking on the big task of building a home. Your project begins with an idea, a hope, a longing of some kind or a wish. Maybe you've spent time looking through magazines, explored home floor plans to find the perfect fit for you, participated in a local home tour or searched the web for hours hoping to find the home that has everything you wanted.

Sadly, some of us don't give ourselves permission to dream, let alone dream big! We believe daydreaming is a creative and significant part of your construction process. Daydreaming gives vision to your dreams. Let your mind wander with the thoughts or ideas regarding your new home or remodeling goals. We have found dreaming big will help you define what it is you really want in the end. Remodeling your American Dream allows you to update your drab kitchen, expand the bathroom to meet the needs of your growing family, or add the home theater, game room or man cave to accommodate your children's (or husband's) friends.

Building a "custom" home to fit your lifestyle, whether it is luxurious, recreational, modern, contemporary, southwestern or whatever you dream up can be liberating. When you build a custom home, you have the freedom to decide every detail, from location to size, overarching style to the finishing touches.

As you build, remodel or update your American Dream, it is important to know why you're doing it. Understanding "Why" you're doing what you're doing is the fuel that powers you through your project. Your "Why" is the key to open the door to the passion needed to start and complete this massive project. The "Why" is the meaning and purpose behind the construction. It will keep you focused on the bigger picture and move you and your significant other toward your goal and each other.

For Lee and Amy, building their own home was about having a project to do together. They wanted to find the perfect acreage in the Black Hills of South Dakota, out in the country where they could have horses, chickens and bunnies. There was abundant wildlife everywhere with hunting, biking and four wheeling opportunities right out their front door.

Their home represented a sanctuary, a place of refuge for family members after a long day's work or school activities. They lived a simple lifestyle, homeschooled their kids and truly enjoyed one another. Therefore, living in the country was ideal for them.

Paperclip Outdoor Living Design Tip: Consider outdoor living. It's a "house beside a house". Outdoor living is added "room" for play, entertainment, reflection or meditation.

In contrast, George and Sami both grew up in communities where the neighborhood kids gathered in the streets each night to play games, where the next door neighbor kids became extended family members. They wanted to create the same kind of memories for their children. As a result, they chose to search out a new construction community that attracted young families like theirs.

What kind of home are you passionate about? Intimately knowing why you're doing what you're doing is the foundation of your house and home. Having the solid understanding of what a home means to you and your spouse, and why it is important to build or remodel, will hold your relationship together as you move forward with your construction process.

2. What Style of Home do You Dream of?

Steve and Leslee were ready to put action to their dream of building a home. Their first step was to hire an architect. They brought pictures to their first meeting with their architect that included what they wanted the kitchen to look like, the layout for the main floor of the home, ideas for the bathroom, elements to be used on the outside of the house and much more. There had been so many styles to choose from, including Cape Cod, Urban Retreat, American Farmhouse, Log Home, and Pueblo.

The architect asked many questions regarding their vision and purpose for their new home. Here are some initial design ideas they imagined in their home.

1. Large south facing windows
2. High ceilings
3. Open floor plan between kitchen and living room
4. Walkout basement
5. A "man cave"

They also wanted a mixture of stone, wood and tile throughout the home that incorporated energy efficient building concepts such as geo thermal heating and cooling. They literally threw all their ideas on the table for discussion and the architect put those ideas into the first draft of their blueprint.

The first review of the draft provided an initial reality check. Steve and Leslee looked over the blueprint detail by detail to evaluate if the blueprint was an accurate representation of what they wanted their home to look like. They made revisions and then submitted the blueprint to their general contractor so he could get a bid together for them. Diagram 1 is an simplified example of the Dream Big, Real Big Process that Steve and Leslee completed with their architect and builder.

Dream Big, Real Big Process
Diagram 1

Dream Big, Real Big-Think and visualize about all you need, want and desire for your project

Example- Large windows, open floor plan between kitchen and living room

Walkout basement, high ceilings, "man cave", 4000 square feet

Initial Reality Check-does this blueprint represent what we had in mind? Where do we need to make changes? Is there anything missing?

Realistic Revisions-Review blueprint with architect/ draftsman, make necessary changes with the architecht

Example: Need a bigger kitchen, master bathroom layout needs some work

Architect/Draftsman reworks the blueprint to reflect your changes.

Second Reality Check- Does the blueprint accurately reflect what you want? If not, keep working at it until you get what you want. Then...

Submit to 3 General Contractors for a bid. If bid doesn't meet your financial goal, rework blueprint until it reflects your goals.

3. Mismatching Dreams

Often couples discover they hold different pictures in their minds of the ideal home. Mike and Jackie, a couple in their mid-life years, were excited to move into Jackie's 1940's vintage home. As they nurtured their relationship they discovered a mutual love for home improvements.

Jackie's home needed serious updates and Mike was eager to get started. They planned on living in this home for one or two more years as Mike established his new business and got to know the area. Then they would determine if they would build or buy a new home.

Both Mike and Jackie were motivated and enthusiastic about their home update project. After all, it would be the first big project they would do together. For months they had talked about different ideas on how they could improve and personalize the house to make it their new home.

Little did they know they would run into problems right off the bat. As the project goals were finalized, Mike wanted to "go all out." He was a handy man and could do a lot of the work himself, believing they would be able to save money.

Jackie was in the interior design business and aware of the general rule of thumb for update and remodel projects—for resale value, don't overbuild for your neighborhood. Jackie wanted to make money on her home she had owned for thirteen years when they went to sell it. She had seen many people put more money into a remodel job than they could get a return on. She did not want to experience that.

Jackie didn't want to squash Mike's passion, but felt compelled to derail some of the projects. She stated her case clearly, but it didn't seem to damper Mike's enthusiasm for spending a lot of money on a lower-end house in a lower-end neighborhood. She felt it wasn't a good use of their funds to over remodel for the neighborhood property value.

This couple, like many, are dreamers with a common goal and interest but with different ideas on how to accomplish it. Sometimes feelings get tied up with goals and then the goals become very personal. It then becomes challenging to think clearly and realistically. Mike and Jackie successfully shared the first part of the Dream Big, Real Big Process with each other but had not gotten the "final reality" check. They were in a standoff.

We worked with Mike and Jackie and led them through the exercise provided at the end of this chapter. Mike recognized his emotions got in the way of logic. He wanted to show Jackie how much he loved her and give her the gift of some new additions in the house. In addition, doing the updates would help Mike feel like it was "their house," not just Jackie's house that he moved in to.

Jackie was very pleased Mike wanted to show his love by doing the entire remodel himself. She also realized she hadn't fully shared her concerns with Mike about over-remodeling. She was afraid to be honest because she didn't want to hurt his feelings. She held back on what she knew was important to her. This was an old behavior that she didn't want to bring in to her new relationship.

After discussing these new discoveries in their relationship, they were willing to move a little slower and to be more honest with one another. Taking one step at a time allowed them to better understand their partner's feelings and motives. In addition, slowing down and reflecting helped them both see they were on the same team working toward the same goals, building a life and home together.

Paperclip Theme Design Tip: The castle of your dreams or the remodeling of your palace would be served very well by being given a title or a theme. Some choices that might fit for you are: Western Contemporary, Rustic Elegance, Urban Loft, Mission with Zen influences, Industrial Modern or a forever favorite, French Country.

What to Do if You're in a Stalemate

If you find yourself in the position of having different ideas on how to achieve your construction goals, here are some suggestions.

1. Independently of one another, prioritize and pick 3 goals or ideas that are important for you.

2. Next, pick only one goal that represents why you wanted to remodel or build.

3. Share this with your partner.

4. Do you see any commonalities you could work toward so both of you feel like it's a win- win?

5. Go to the end of this chapter and answer the questions and share with your partner. See if this might help.

6. If you're still stuck and things don't feel right, go to Key 3, Let Your Needs and Values be Your Guide. Read it and complete the reflection questions and come back to your goals and see if things might have changed.

If you still feel like you're in a standoff, don't worry! Here's a summary. Review your Dream Big, Real Big Process and identify your top priorities. Share with your partner and look for the similarities, not the differences. Answer all Key Reflection questions and complete any activities in the book so far. It may help you to just read ahead and come back to this section of the book, as further information may help with your stalemate.

Whether you and your spouse have similar dreams and goals, or you have diverse goals, we want you to know that the Dream Big, Real Big Process is extremely important to you getting the results you want for your remodel job or newly built home. It can make the difference between having regrets and feeling fully satisfied with your home.

> *"The future belongs to those who believe in the beauty of their dreams."*
> ~Eleanor Roosevelt

Exercises:

Take a look at our many suggestions below and select the one or ones that best suit you as a couple. You will be most able to co-create a home that fits your needs as a couple if you take time to dream and share your vision with your partner. If you share the same dream at the beginning, you will run into fewer problems and be able to make better decisions together during the process.

1. Dream Big, Real Big Process

Take 15 minutes and just dream about what it is you want in your remodeling or ground-up building project. Do this on a separate piece of paper, utilize the space below or go to Appendix A. Dream Big, Real Big. Get creative and let the juices flow. Don't worry about finances or think about if your idea is realistic. Diagram 2 in Appendix A is blank so you can make multiple copies for use in your Dream Big, Real Big Process.

- **Think and visualize about all you need, want and desire for your project. Write in space below**

- Initial Reality Check-does this blueprint represent what we had in mind? Where do we need to make changes? Is there anything missing?

- Architect/Draftsman reworks the blueprint to reflect your changes.

- The end result is an agreement between all parties that this is the plan to follow. There is a feeling of peace about moving forward.

2. Dream Board

Make a dream board together. But first make one of your own. He makes his, she makes hers. Cut pictures out of magazines that inspire you in regards to building your house. Take photos of objects and situations that move you. You might even draw something you love. Anything is good as long as it addresses your new life in your new home together.

Will there be horses and a lot of pasture, or a high rise? Are there kids and pets? How about a piano bar and a jukebox? The sky is the limit! Dream big! Then, with discussion, edit together your individual boards, a little of his and a little of hers into a third one – a blended board. Find a few things together to add to the third board and you're done. Put it on the wall or on an easel. Look at it often as you get ready to build. Tweak it as time goes on.

3. Visit Other Homes

Go to a Parade of Homes in your community or take a weekend trip to another city to see their Parade of Homes. You'll get gain useful ideas and a lot of information. They are a great visual tool and create discussion. Parades are usually in the spring and fall.

4. Home Shows

 Go to Home Shows near and far! Take in the seminars they offer. This is fun and easy to do together.

5. Test Your Knowledge of Your Partner

The next time you are together in a big-box home project store, go to the wall paint samples. In one minute only, each of you pick your favorite six paint colors. Do this exercise alone, no guidance or noises from your beloved. Then talk about each other's choices. This usually results in a lively discussion. You'll be surprised what you learn about the other's choices – or not! ("Let's just paint everything white.")

6. Talk to Experienced Home Owners

Go out to dinner with friends who have already built a home. Choose trustworthy friends who are fairly close to you. Share in detail your dreams about building. Try to pick a couple that has been through the process and listen to their experiences, the good, the bad and the ugly. Wine helps!

7. Childhood Memories

Share childhood memories about the houses you lived in. What, if anything, would you like to bring forward (i.e. the big porch) into your dream home? What absolutely can never show up in your new house?

8. Make a Joint Decorating Decision

Together, buy a piece of furniture that doesn't at all work in your current home. (I visualize a big cabinet.) But you both know you will love it in your new house. Put it in a rather conspicuous place as a reminder that one way or another, you're going to get that house built so you can place that piece of furniture in the right location. You're tired of stubbing your toes on it!

9. Count your blessings

Discuss what you are grateful for, laugh out loud and hold each other close!! This is quite a journey you're on!

ADDITIONAL EXERCISES FOR COUPLES
WHO ARE BUILDING A NEW HOME

1. Check Out the Area of Your New Home

Go grocery shopping, get fuel for the car, go to church, and go to a movie close to where your new house could be or will be built. It sends messages to your brain that you're already there.

2. Detach from Your Current Home

Begin the not so fun stuff. Disengage some from your current house by purging! It has to be done. You have time to do this in small bites. Reward yourselves heavily every time you spend two hours together at this task.

Reflection Questions

In addition to the Dream Big, Real Big Process and diagram, the exercises below offer thought provoking questions to contemplate and help you take a deeper look into the reasons for doing what you're doing or the "why's" fueling your decisions. These questions can help you determine if it's the right time to build or remodel.

- What's the difference between a house and home?

- What does my home represent to me?

- What will my home give me?

- Why am I building or remodeling? Now?

- How would I feel if I didn't build or remodel now?

- What are the emotion(s) I am experiencing as I consider these questions?

*"A good plan is like a road map:
it shows the final destination and usually
the best way to get there."*

~H Stanley Judd

 **Key Three:**

Let Your Needs and Values be Your Guide

ABLUEPRINT, GPS, MAP, COMPASS, ROAD, PATH, and True North provide direction. A blueprint will help you successfully build or remodel your home. It guides your builder.

Your car GPS will talk to you and tell you when to take a right or left to get you to a new restaurant. That good old fashion map made of paper can help you find your way on those poorly marked four-wheel trails in the Black Hills of South Dakota. The tried and true compass helps backpackers of the Shenandoah National Park navigate their way around those beautiful mountains without getting lost. The road from home to the grocery store takes you where you need to go. A deer path in the woods allows a hunter to follow the deer he has been tracking for hours.

In Asia, an ordinary person drops a small shard of iron onto a leaf and watches as the leaf floats on the water. Without explanation, the leaf spins around until it points in the same direction every time. Historians and archeologists believe this is how the compass, the original navigational tool, was discovered.

"True North" is a term used in a variety of ways. People in the world of navigation say, "True North is a geographical direction represented on maps and globes by lines of longitude. Each line of longitude begins and ends at the Earth's poles and represents direct north and south travel." Finding True North is very important to find if you are looking how to get from one place to the next.

In the helping profession and leadership circles, True North is described as your personal needs and values that guide your life decisions. God made you this way! It's what makes you unique and different from the next person.

It's Easy to Get Lost in a Project

Without a clear plan based in your dreams, needs and values, you will likely get sidetracked, distracted or even lost.

Nathan and Ami, the newlywed couple who argued about granite counter tops and how many outlets to put in the house had a very loose construction plan. They originally budgeted $75,000 for the full remodel job. Nathan had purchased the home prior to getting married and he wanted the best for his new wife and unborn baby. Before they knew it, Nathan and Ami had blown through the $75K long before the finishing touches Ami wanted, like new furniture and window treatments. They did not break down the costs item by item. Instead they had generalities of $30,000 for the kitchen, $10,000 for the entryway, flooring $20,000, etc. It was too general; they lacked a clear, well thought out plan.

Nathan and Ami had a seven day old baby when Ami was out selecting kitchen cabinets as they were under a time crunch for ordering. Ami was on automatic pilot, tired, overwhelmed and disengaged from the remodel project due to having a newborn baby. She was vulnerable and resentful because she didn't have control of her time, the budget or vision for the project. She was new to married life and a first time mom. The timing of this was a train wreck!

Paperclip Kitchen Design Tip: You are a good candidate for Granite counter tops if you appreciate what comes from the earth as it is. Granite is almost impossible to micromanage but ask the fabricator if they can place less beautiful sections in lesser-seen places. Sometimes they can.

Nathan and Ami were off course. Instead of enjoying their remodel project, new life together and new baby, their marriage was full of stress, discord and resentment. This stemmed from not starting with a blueprint, plan of action or personal introspection on the deeper meaning of their project.

Having a clear plan that provides thought out steps to help you achieve your goal can be the difference between enjoying and celebrating the success of building or remodeling your home or strife, anxiety and regret.

Your Needs and Values

Be energized and motivated by your uniqueness. Combine that with dreams that need fulfillment and you have a blueprint for joy and success. If you want to live life to the fullest, take a deeper look into what your needs and values are by completing the questionnaire at the end of the chapter. Cheryl Weir and Associates designed this questionnaire for leadership purposes; it can help you discover new levels within yourself and others around you. You're in a leadership role if you're remodeling or building so you will benefit immensely if you take the time to complete the questionnaire.

Here's a simple overview. Cheryl describes needs as "things, conditions and feelings you must have to be minimally satisfied in life." When needs aren't met, they "scream" at you or you may feel stuck. Like when you're starving (need), your stomach growls at you. Once you feed yourself, your stomach won't growl or scream at you. Once your need is met, it won't demand your attention.

Your needs can change throughout your life. They can appear as a result of change such as a job loss, death, birth of a child . . . or a transition such as building, remodeling, aging or illness. Anytime you are going through a change or some sort of transition, new needs may appear.

Jim and Nancy were trying to live in their home while they were remodeling. At one point, Jim became overwhelmed and started arguing with his wife. Jim was not normally the argumentative type. After discussing his outburst with Nancy they realized they needed to find order and harmony in their life. Their whole house, except the master bedroom, was being remodeled so there was no order in their home; thus, the tension and argument.

Because Jim and Nancy knew their needs, they were able to focus on getting the order/harmony need met instead of going at each other. They decided to move in with their daughter for a few weeks to get a break from the chaos of their home. They avoided more potential misunderstandings by addressing Jim's unmet need of order and harmony.

Cheryl says "Values are who you are. Values are not something you need." They're your unique personality. Once your needs are meet you can flourish and express yourself through your values. Values typically don't change. They express your essence.

When you honor yourself by living your values, there is a sense of "rightness" about life. Values are crucial when decision making times arise, and in times of adversity. When you are completely aware and embrace your values, you are able to respond appropriately and without delay.

"When we are motivated by goals that have deep meaning, by dreams that need completion, by pure love that needs expressing, then we truly live life."
~ Greg Anderson

When Mike and Neda were building their home, they knew the value of learning is at the heart of their family. Their children were early elementary school age and they home schooled their kids. Therefore, they focused more time designing the schoolroom and spent more money in this part of the house than some others. They used this room on a daily basis and it offered the whole family a place of inspired learning.

Tim and Susan were in the final stages of remodeling their kitchen. They had waited two weeks for a unique, handmade countertop for their kitchen island. Once it arrived, they noticed it had a scratch in a prominent place. They had a decision to make, as the countertop was already weeks late and they had a big party planned at their house in two days.

Because Susan liked things done right and wanted the countertop to look its best, she wanted the countertop taken back to the shop to be done correctly. Tim had planned this party for his daughter and couldn't change the date. He was devastated because he didn't think they could have the party because the kitchen island (in a prominent location) wasn't going to be usable. With some creative problem solving, they were able to come up with a temporary solution to the countertop and have the party. They decided together that Susan's value of Mastery (having things done right) took precedent over having a countertop for the party. Having the countertop done right in the bigger picture was what they both really wanted.

Now, another couple could have handled this situation totally different. For illustration purposes, let's say John was really artsy and had a creative flair to life. An imperfection in the countertop did not bother him at all. In fact, he claimed "it adds character to the countertop." Mary loved to entertain and wanted to have the party no matter what. They both could live with the countertop just the way it was.

> **Paperclip Interior Designer Tip:** Hire an interior designer who knows the design rules and how and when to break them. Trust them to use an internal compass to navigate through the vision you have of your new home.

We suggest you and your spouse go ahead and take the Needs and Value Questionnaire in Appendix B. Do it now before reading anymore of this chapter. It is well worth the time it takes to complete it. We promise it will help you and your home construction process! Be sure to read the scoring instructions thoroughly before beginning.

1. Write your top 3 Needs here:

2. Write your top 3 Values here:

3. Write your spouse's top 3 Needs here:

4. Write your spouse's top 3 Values here:

Now that you know your needs and values, go back to your Dream Big, Real Big Process, Dream Board or other dreaming tool you used and evaluate how your needs and values are embodied in your building or remodeling vision. The goal is to have your needs and values fully reflected in your project. If this connection is a little off, go back and create plans or ideas that totally express and reveal who you both are.

No Right or Wrong

There is no right or wrong, as each couple has unique needs and values. It's more about working with one another, not against each other. When decisions need to be made, let your needs and values guide and direct you. It's OK to take some time to run your choices through the grid of your individual needs and values and how they impact your coupleship. The benefit of aligning your life with your core needs and values is that two things are released; incredible creativity, immense satisfaction.

Your unique needs and values are your personal compass. Fulfilling and respecting these needs and values in your relationship will guide your coupleship with ease toward those things that are important to you, like your home. Dreaming big and incorporating your needs and values into this dream is a recipe for a full life. Your needs and values will help you choose those details and ideas in your home that are extremely important to you.

Tom and Jeanie both had the "need" to Work and shared the "values" of Adventure and Mastery as described in the Needs and Values Questionnaire. They both like physical work and enjoy being busy. Jeanie liked the idea of doing some of the remodel work themselves as this would be risky for her and she likes to walk into unknown projects or activities. Tom likes to work with his hands and likes things to be their best. He takes pride in doing his projects with excellence.

They talked through their remaining needs and values to determine if there could be problems moving forward. They recognized that neither of them had remodeled or built anything before but they were excited to take on such a task. They were fortunate that they started with a small project and were able to experience great success!

Your personal compass, map, blueprint or GPS will impact the direction of the relationship and the outcome of your building project. It doesn't matter if you like a map, GPS or blueprint better; the important thing is to have a tool that guides you, helps you stay on track and assists you in making wise decisions. It could save your relationship.

The Master Interior Design Plan

Now we want you to have fun, be creative and feel inspired with interior design tips. Here is a Master Interior Design Plan you can use to layout and shape your new Living Room or Great Room. In addition, you can use this structure for planning the other rooms in your home. Before you commit to or buy anything for the living room, have your Master Plan set in your mind and on paper. One decision hinges on another, so slow down and allow yourself the discipline of putting it together in this order. It is helpful to visualize these steps completed.

1. Pick the overall theme of your room. What emotionally speaks to you?

2. Consider what will be your focal point. Where is it in the room? Make a template of the furniture layout around your focal point. Try to have a primary and secondary seating area.

3. Make your lighting plan. Plan for lamp light to be in a triangle(s) around the room. Pay attention to your probable need for floor outlets. Cords running from the center of the room to the nearest wall outlet can be avoided. Layer your lighting: ceiling, walls and lamp light.

4. Choose your color scheme. Refer back to the color wheel for guidance. Hear this: have fun, loosen up and be playful with color! Breathe and trust your inner designer/artist. Color is your opportunity to express yourself and to make a positive emotional impact in your home. You get a lot of look for the money with a gallon of paint.

Paperclip Color Design Tip: Enjoy color!! You get a lot of look for the money with a gallon of paint.

5. Consider flooring options. The flooring industry has exploded with options. Lay out three groups of three choices to keep narrowing down your selections. You may have several rounds of this process. Stay with it, you won't be sorry. Knowledge is power in choosing your floor surfaces.

6. Choose and co-ordinate flooring, wall color/ special wall treatments and upholstery at the same time. Hang in there! This room is starting to rock!

7. Choose tables and accent pieces. Your theme will drive your choices. Mix shapes, sizes, old and new pieces to keep the room from being "too tight" in your theme.

8. Chose lamps and lighting styles. Place a really fun, unexpected lamp in the room just for kicks and conversation. Remember the leg lamp in The Christmas Story movie? (You don't have to go that far!) If you have five lamps in a room, two should match.

Paperclip Electric Design Tip: People often believe you should try to lighten up a dark area in your home with a light paint. However, the way to lighten up a room is with electrical power! If you paint a dull room a light color, you will probably end up with a dull gray room. If you paint a dark area in a rich color – red, for instance, its darkness takes on inviting warmth. Darkness itself is not a bad thing.

9. Choose window treatments. I believe window treatments should be low key and subordinate to the rest of the room.

10. Choose accessories. Use odd numbers. The trend is for fewer, but larger pieces. Use mixtures of textures and elements: glass, metal, water and wood for example. Scale is important in how pieces relate to each other when placed together. For example, don't place a very tall piece next to a very short piece.

Make your choices from a place of joy, not fear, and you will have an excellent outcome. Trust that little voice inside you that supports you in creating your room. Do this and your room will feed you emotionally. Good luck!!!

Reflection Questions and Activities

- Complete Needs and Values Questionnaire (See Appendix B)

- Share findings with spouse, discuss commonalities and differences

- Post your Needs and Values in a prominent place so you can keep your eyes on what's important

- Get started on your Master Interior Design Plan

"Maybe that's what it all comes down to. Love, not as a surge of passion, but as a choice to commit to something, someone, no matter what obstacles or temptations stand in the way. And maybe making that choice, again and again, day in and day out, year after year, says more about love than never having a choice to make at all."

~Emily Giffin, *Love the One You're With*

 **Key Four:**

Plan Sensibly

YOU HAVE HAD THE OPPORTUNITY TO DREAM UP a shared vision of your home that incorporates your needs and values. Now it's time to translate those wonderful ideas into financial realities so you will have a realistic and achievable plan of action.

If you played with the Dream Big, Real Big Process. you have a well-defined vision of what you want in your home. By this time your unique needs and values are set in motion to guide your decisions through the numerous choices to be made in home construction. You've carefully chosen the people and resources that will work with you throughout your project.

Now you've arrived at a critical intersection in the building or remodeling process. It's time to see if your vision can be supported financially. This is where the rubber hits the road and financial reality is exposed. Having a construction bid on your project helps align your home construction vision with your budget. Did we just say the "B" word?

The "B" Word

Budget. The "B" word that most people don't like. In fact, most people have some kind of visceral response to the word "budget." Did you? Did you feel that knot in your stomach or experience a sensation of dread? Maybe you thought "I don't need a budget, a ball park idea is good enough for us."

Perhaps you're one of those people who love to crunch numbers and like having a budget? If so, when I mentioned the word "budget," you probably got excited—you will really appreciate this chapter!

Most couples fall somewhere between knowing they need a budget to avoidance of the issue. We feel having a budget is vital to the success of your project. Try this next exercise with your spouse to gain a greater understanding of how your beliefs about budgeting can impact your project.

On a piece of paper write the word "budget" at the top. Or use the space below to write the thoughts and feelings you have about following a budget. I know, you really don't want to do this exercise, but it is worth the effort. Do this together with your partner. Come on, don't cheat yourself or the success of your project!

Here are a few beliefs we have heard from others who have done this exercise before: "Budgets are too much work", "It takes too long to set one up", "there are too many unknowns", I don't even know where to start!" You may feel a variety of emotions such as anxiety, overwhelm, anger, hurt, resentment, fear or shame.

Budget

Thoughts	Feelings
"Confining"	"Uneasy"

Did you notice anything about the above thoughts and feelings? Most of the responses were negative. That is typically what we experience with people in general around the topic of money and budgets. Budgets have a bad reputation.

Because of the financial melt down in the United States that began in 2008, many have needed to reassess and re-evaluate their finances. It's been a tough ride for a lot of Americans and financial changes have been made on many levels. One positive outcome of such turmoil is the media coverage and Internet access regarding money management.

If you think about it, budgets are just a set or sequence of numbers on a piece of paper or in an excel spreadsheet. A budget is an inanimate object. However, budgets are tied to money and the topic of money can feel perplexing or even like a taboo subject. (Unless your one of those people who love to number crunch! Then you will probably find this topic inspiring and motivating.)

It can be difficult for people to have honest, empowering and healthy discussions regarding money. It's really not about the money; it's more about what money represents. Because of this, your relationship conversations around money can become tricky.

We want to help change this so you can experience freedom and be empowered to achieve your construction goals. Awareness of your own experience with budgeting, attention to your thoughts and a consciousness to your feelings in regards to budgeting will help you have a positive experience.

Having a clearly defined budget can save you from having unnecessary arguments in your relationship and control costs. A home building/remodel budget is a financial plan for your entire process. The primary purpose of developing a budget is to understand and control costs. It is meant to be a guide so you don't overspend. It's really your financial blueprint, your financial GPS or financial map of intention. There are a lot of names for it. Pick one that feels good and right for you.

The key is to match the reasons you're building or remodeling (Keys 1 & 2) with your needs and values (Key 3) and transform that into a reality based financial plan. Occasionally they match up, sometimes they're close and every so often they are way off.

Having a realistic plan on how to spend money on your home is another cornerstone to having a successful building project. If you Google the number one reason for divorce, you will often find money problems at the top of the list. If the topic of money causes strife in your marriage and you decide to add the stress of building or remodeling, you may be creating a blueprint for disaster.

Most people in relationships have different ways of handling money. If you think about your partner and their relationship with money, it's most likely different than yours. Maybe significantly different. Olivia Mellan, a psychotherapist and business consultant in the field of money conflict resolution, works with couples around their relationship with money. She has observed some interesting dynamics between couples. In her book *Money Harmony: A Road Map for Individuals and Couples,* she identifies how your history with money impacts your current relationship with money. She helps you pinpoint your money personalities, recognize your money myths and how this impacts your relationship. You can actually take the quiz for free on her web site. (http://www.moneyharmony.com/MHQuiz.html)

Paperclip 20% Tip: Put an additional 20% of your budget in a separate account to use in emergencies only.

Opposites Attract

Many couples polarize and get stuck in the way they handle or talk about money. Matt and Cindy are an example of polarization in a marriage. Opposites attract. Matt was a money avoider; he didn't like dealing with money most of the time. He could take it or leave it. Cindy on the other hand, was a worrier. She thought about it all day long. She worried about how they were going to pay the phone bill, or how they would pay for their children's college someday. Cindy was also extremely worried about how they were going to afford the current house they were building.

Most people get into a relationship with someone who is almost the complete opposite of them. This is one of the natural phenomena's where nature seeks balance. Hoarders marry spenders, risk takers will get into a relationship with a risk avoider, and so on. Over time, these polarizations become more rigid where frustration and conflict rule the relationship.

Matt and Cindy had built two previous homes. They were forced to sell each home after they finished building because they couldn't afford to live in them. As you can imagine, Sandy was surprised when she got a call to help build their third home.

The focus of Sandy's work in this home was to help design the girls' bedrooms. Matt and Cindy had a blended family with his kids, her kids and their kid. The preteen girls were Matt's kids from his previous marriage. It was important for their bedrooms to be special because, as divorced kids, they moved from mom's home to dad's home on a weekly basis. Cindy really longed for the girls to "want" to come to their home. Thus, Cindy and Sandy spent a lot of time and money decorating their rooms.

One of the unique things about being an interior designer (as well as working as a therapist and life coach) is that people open up and talk about lots of issues. Sandy spends a good portion of time with people as they work on their project together, so she hears their personal struggles. Cindy would often share her financial worries with Sandy. Cindy stated she was concerned about how much money they were pouring into this new house. She disclosed to Sandy that she had recently inherited money and she resented that they were using her inheritance to build this home. They had already lost two previous homes and could not effectively talk about money without the conversation erupting into an argument.

In fact, they did not build a budget with the current home, nor the previous two. This time, Matt and Cindy had an "allowance" because of the inheritance amount, but did not have an itemized budget to follow. Thus, Cindy was concerned they wouldn't be able to finish the house because they would run out of money. In the worst-case scenario, they would have to move out of this home, too. She just couldn't go through that one more time!

Eventually, Cindy's worst fears did come true, they lost the new home and filed for bankruptcy. This may have been avoided if they could have had open, realistic and productive conversations on the subject of money, had good conflict resolution skills and developed a budget and lived within this budget.

As you can sense when reading this story, the problems in this relationship were much bigger than the money. Relationships are complicated and struggles can run deep. We aren't here to judge or bring shame upon Matt and Cindy. We just want to learn from the mistakes in order to support you in taking steps to be successful and sustain your relationship while remodeling or building.

Having a budget designed together based upon your needs, values, goals *and* within your financial boundaries will help you achieve your home building goals.

Paperclip Flooring Design Tip: Often times, your builder doesn't budget enough for flooring. It's often way too low, so budget more in than you think.

Before we move onto the "how-to's" of making a budget, take some time to answer these questions and then talk about them together. The questions may help you understand your relationship with money so you can make conscious, healthy decisions for your coupleship and building project.

1. What is your earliest memory about money?

2. What is your happiest memory with money?

3. What is an unhappy memory concerning money?

4. How did your parents handle money?

5. How would you describe yourself with money? (i.e. giver, thrifty, stingy, careless)

What words do you associate with money? For example, some people might think money equals power. Fill in the blanks.

Money =_____

Money =_____

Money =_____

Money =_____

As you look at your responses to these questions, what conclusions can you draw about how you feel about money? What are some of the events that have shaped your money beliefs? Do these beliefs help or hinder your relationship with money and a significant other?

In his book *Conscious Finance,* Rick Kahler helps readers discover their money beliefs. He believes when you truly know how your money beliefs influence your life you are on the road to being financially conscious. Therefore, you are able to make healthier decisions. Being aware of money beliefs and how they block your goals, or painfully influence your daily lives, can help you avoid disaster. Awareness is the next step to making useful, conscious decisions that move you toward your home construction and life goals.

We all have money beliefs. Some serve you well, others may get in the way of you adequately using money as the tool it is. For example, "Buy only used items because they will be cheaper," is a money belief Terry firmly believed was best for his family. He bought used clothing for his four kids, he purchased used cars, and his used lawn mower had lasted well over twenty years.

Terry was able to save some money on his remodel job when he found a great deal on lighting for his bathroom, a used toilet that was in good shape, and a sink that matched the toilet color. He was very excited about these finds. Unfortunately, he had multiple problems with all three items within the first six months of completing his remodel project. He was able to fix a few of the problems but ended up having to purchase new light fixtures. Which in the end cost him more money than if he bought the light at retail value. This is one example of how a money belief can cause problems.

Money beliefs can be partially true and to some extent be incorrect. Part of Terry's money belief is true in that you can

> "A belief is not merely an idea the mind posses; it's an idea that possess the mind".
> ~Robert Balton

save money when buying used items. On the other hand, it can end up costing more money in the long run because the items don't function properly. A new item, sometimes full priced, needs to be purchased to replace the faulty item.

Another example of a partially true belief is "You have to work hard for your money." Sometimes this is true as some hardworking people make good money. And some people don't work hard or don't work at all and have money. Are you getting the idea here?

Money beliefs are not all good or all bad. The idea is to identify your money beliefs and assess if they are helping you. Do they assist you in achieving your goals or do they inhibit you in any way? There are no right or wrong answers. Know your beliefs, and those of your spouse, and then work together to strengthen the beliefs that work for your situation and let go of those beliefs constrain you. Sometimes this can be very, very difficult. If you get stuck, you may need additional help. This would be a good time to get help from a therapist (such as Laura Longville) who understands money beliefs.

How to Develop a Budget

Great work! You identified your thoughts and feelings around budgeting, you know how your money beliefs impact your life and how they will influence your relationship. You are more equipped to move ahead in creating a budget that will fully serve you and your project. There are multiple ways to do this. The bookshelves are full of advice and the Internet is overflowing with information. If you are working with a builder, they will walk you through this. As you do your research you will begin to find some commonalities. Having a budget is number one on your list PRIOR to starting, or even committing, to your project.

Most of you will need to go to the bank and see how much the bank will loan for your remodel or building plan. In general, you will qualify for more "house" than you can really afford. There are all sorts of recommendations on how much your home costs should be in relation to your overall living costs. Please do your research and seek wise counsel on this. Here are a couple of examples from Credit.com and Crown. org respectively.

"Mortgage lenders have traditionally expected borrowers to have a **housing expense ratio** of 28% or less. The housing expense ratio is an indication of a borrower's ability to make the payments on their mortgage loan. The ratio measures housing expense as a percentage of gross income (income before deducting for Social Security, Medicare, and taxes). For example, if a borrower's salary were $4,000 per month, a lender would approve their loan if the housing expense - mortgage payment, fire insurance, and property taxes - were less than $1,120 per month. $1,120/$4,000 = 0.28.

"In addition to the housing expense ratio, lenders also consider a borrower's total expenses, housing expenses, plus fixed monthly obligations. By traditional lending standards, total expenses could not exceed 36% of gross income. In other words, continuing the previous example, a borrower with housing expenses of $1,120 per month and fixed monthly bills of $350 would have $1,470 in total expenses per month. The **total expense ratio** would be 36.75% ($1,470/$4,000 = .3675), and the lender would not approve the loan."

The late Larry Burkett taught budgeting using the Net Spendable Income (NSI). NSI is what is left after giving and taxes. "There are three primary categories in every person' budget: Housing, Food and Auto. If these three combined percentages exceed 70 percent of your NSI, then it will be almost impossible to have a balanced budget. Example: Housing 38%, Food and Auto each14% of your NSI.

The average person usually has no idea how much he or she is spending annually or monthly. The first step, then, is to track what you spend and compare it to the guidelines shown here. Only then should you begin to adjust your budget to make it balance. For some it may mean selling assets to pay down debt, and for others it may mean seeking assistance with debt reduction from a trained counselor. Still others may find that they have surpluses in areas of their budget. For them the challenge is deciding where to allocate this surplus: to retirement, college planning, or increased giving."

There are many resources available today to help you create and maintain a balanced budget. It is wise to get your financial house in order prior to taking on new home construction or remodeling endeavor.

If you are fortunate and don't need a loan, it is still wise to determine how much money you want to spend on your project. As you're reflecting on this, let your needs, values, and dreams guide your decision. Once you have determined how much money you have to work with, you can begin.

Start with getting three bids for your remodel or building project. It is good to have choice and not be tied to an "either, or" option. It is important to get as much detail on the costs as possible up front. This will help reduce the amount of surprises or unexpected costs that come up.

The bid you pick should reflect your needs, values and goals. If not, go back to your needs and values and let them be your guides. Align them with your goals. It is wise to spend some time on this as you want to make sure the bid reflects your desires. It may take some negotiation between you and your spouse to get it just right. But take the extra time to do this as it sets the foundation for everything else.

"We can tell our values by looking at our checkbook stubs."
~Gloria Steinem

In our experience it is beneficial for you to have a separate category in your budget allowing for an overage of 20%. This is a cushion in your budget that is only to be used in extreme situations such as unexpected land development issues. For example, drilling a well can often times be unpredictable. Or it can be a bunch of little things that add up, such as change orders initiated by the homeowners. Examples include and not limited to moving walls, adding windows or changing electrical outlets and switches. These changes take manpower linked to paying someone to make those changes. Cha Ching!

Put this "plus 20%" in a separate account if possible, don't think about or plan to use it. It's there for emergency or unexpected costs.

It is sensible to get budget reports or updates throughout your project from your General Contractor so you can understand where you are at with your spending. If you are a DIY'er or your own GC, stay on top of your costs and assess whether or not you are following your budget. Make necessary adjustments as needed. If you are faithful in doing this you can control your costs and guide your project into successful completion.

"Money harmony must come from within. It cannot be bought simply by acquiring more money"

~Olivia Mellan

 **Key Five:**

Live in Financial Integrity

HAVING A BUDGET IS NECESSARY FOR KEEPING your relationship on solid ground during the building or remodeling process. But having a budget isn't enough—you and your partner must follow that budget together for the best possible outcome. If the topic of money causes strife in your marriage and then you add the stress of building or remodeling; it could be a blueprint for disaster. We are devoting an entire chapter to financial integrity because we've seen couples, time and again, suffer the consequences of mismanaging their spending.

What does it mean to have financial integrity? The simplest definition: be honest. Be honest with yourself, your partner, and faithful with your money. Live honorably, be reliable, truthful and follow your financial plan.

Most people in relationships have different ways of handling money. This can cause discomfort, friction and disagreements. You probably discovered in the last chapter that your money beliefs differ from your partner's. Differences are to be expected and can be discussed and resolved.

Financial Infidelity

The opposite of integrity is infidelity. Most of you know what infidelity is. We hear about it all the time in the media, people write songs about it, and many a heart is broken because of it. We usually think of infidelity as one person stepping outside of the relationship, through an emotional or sexual affair. Believe it or not, this can happen with money as well.

Financial infidelity is when people are dishonest, unfaithful or disloyal with money. Most often, financial infidelity involves one partner making financial decisions independently and trying to keep those decisions secret. Jeff and Patty hired Sandy to help them redesign the exterior grounds of their Tudor style home. This involved rock walls, a metal lattis archway and brick pathways. They spent a lot of time putting together a design and a plan. Sandy met with the contractors and the work began.

Unbeknown to both Patty and Sandy, Jeff changed a lot of the agreed upon plan. He met with the contractors by himself and made changes. He didn't talk with Patty nor consult with Sandy first. Confusion, discord and anger were felt once Jeff's dishonesty and betrayal

> *"Lies and secrets are like a cancer in the soul. They eat away what is good and leave only destruction behind."*
>
> ~Cassandra Clare, *Clockwork Prince*

regarding the original budget and design plan was discovered.

Jeff's independent decisions created a wave of disaster. It is very hard to "re-do" rock walls, mortar and color-treated concrete, stay within budget and keep all parties satisfied. The contractors walked off the job, Patty felt extremely betrayed by her husband and Sandy couldn't work with such disarray and conflict in her client's marriage.

The Danger of Secrets

Secrets are, by definition, hidden. We hide them in various places or stuff them away not to be found by anyone. You, or I might even forget where we put them. Sometimes, secrets are shoved under the bed; soon they swell and leak out into view. Other times, we throw secrets into corners and underneath dirty laundry, and they really start to stink. Occasionally our spouse or friends go looking for an "item" and end up finding the very thing we were trying to hide. Either way, it's extremely uncomfortable and secrecy destroys relationships.

Given that we have complex relationships with people and money, it is not shocking people keep secrets. Leading financial psychologists, Drs. Ted and Brad Klontz state "when secrecy or dishonesty over money persists in a relationship, it can become the disorder we call financial infidelity—deliberately and surreptitiously keeping a major secret about one's spending or finances from one's partner."

Sandy worked with Rich and Kate, both known as hard workers in their professions. They had two young children and were ecstatic about building their dream home. Sandy helped them through their building process, from the blueprint stage to placing the last accessories.

Rich and Kate were actively involved in the building process. Kate was a little more involved with the interior design and Rich with the overall financial aspects of the project. In addition, Rich really enjoyed the "hands on" part of the décor decisions.

It became sticky for Sandy in the final interior design phase. They were planning and selecting window treatments, furniture and final accessories. Kate asked Sandy to submit two different invoices for these items. A statement reflecting the accurate costs was provided to Kate, and to Rich a less than truthful invoice was provided. Kate's reasoning was "it would be easier this way and after all, I work hard for my money."

Sandy felt she was in no place to judge what was going on and wanted to complete the project. Therefore, she did what was asked by providing two different invoices. Like Sandy and Laura, this story may leave you feeling anxious or uncomfortable.

We don't know the deeper reasons why Kate wanted the money handled this way, though we have a few ideas on why people are dishonest with money. In the helping profession, there is a saying "You are as sick as the secrets you keep." If you don't talk about how you think or feel openly and honestly then you are hiding or withholding. When we hide something it usually goes to a place we can't see it or find it.

Kate keeping a secret about the "real" costs of the window treatments, furniture and accessories from Rich is an example of financial infidelity. Infidelity of any kind rocks the foundation of a relationship. Financial infidelity when building or remodeling can destroy the structure of your home and marriage. Financial infidelity includes lying about the costs of big-ticket items or secrets about major purchases outside the pre-determined budget. Other examples of financial infidelity could include cashing out an IRA, taking out a second mortgage or using gifted money without the knowledge of your spouse.

We don't know if Rich ever found out about Kate's infidelity but if he had he may ask himself "If she is lying to me about this, what else is she lying to me about?" If the infidelity is not uncovered, secrecy and deceit create an unsafe, endangered relationship.

The undermining and deceit in these two examples had nothing to do with their construction goals. They represent much deeper issues in the people and the relationship. Most of the time, financial infidelity has nothing to do with money. Lack of trust may be at the core of the relationship. Often, lying or being deceitful stems from trust issues in childhood. At times people withhold information, are dishonest, or keep secrets because they are afraid of the response from their spouse. Maybe it's the real or anticipated anger or fear of rejection from their spouse where dishonesty takes root. Secrecy, dishonesty, trickery, deceit, or whatever you want to call it, destroys the integrity of relationships.

This is a reminder that the issues present in a relationship prior to building or remodeling will be revealed during the project. No one is exempt from this. Our hope is that you use this as an opportunity to grow, change, nurture your relationship, achieve your home construction goals and keep the love in your relationship.

The S.A.F.E Way to Deal with Money

If you find yourself in this situation, where you are the one instigating financial infidelity or suspect you are being lied to, then do something. In their book, *Mind Over Money, Overcoming the Money Disorders That Threaten Our Financial Health,* Rick Kahler, Drs. Ted and Brad Klontz developed a four-step process to help couples address financial infidelity. It uses the acronym SAFE.

S: Speak Your Truth—Be honest. It's the best place to start rebuilding the foundation of financial safety in your relationship.

A: Agree to a Plan—A spending plan (aka budget) is a healthy component of a financially healthy relationship and will help you build or remodel productively while, strengthening the bond of trust, safety and love in your marriage.

F: Follow the Agreement—This is the hard part. That's why it's imperative to take the time to develop a solid budget. It will still be challenging at times to actually follow the spending plan but it is easier if you have a well thought out budget developed by you, your spouse and your contractor as you begin. There will be unexpected things happen and we will help you deal with this in Key 6.

E: Establish an Emergency Response Plan—Sometimes couples can't talk about money without fighting, can't come to any agreement or follow through with the plan. They could be in trouble and not just about money. An emergency plan is for those times when all else fails. It helps the couple have a "next step." This next step could include seeking help from a pastor, therapist, psychologist or marriage and family therapist.

Following the SAFE plan can prepare and smooth your construction process and provide a stronger relationship bond. The plan is what keeps you on the same side, working together. When there isn't a well thought out, pre-agreed upon plan, your partner can

> *"Real integrity is doing the right thing, knowing that nobody's going to know whether you did it or not."*
> ~Oprah Winfrey

feel like your enemy. You don't need your spouse to be your enemy.

The use of the term "financial infidelity" may give the impression that one partner is deceiving the other partner. This isn't always the case.

We've worked with couples that give lip service to their budget and then make mutual decisions without consulting their plan. Both people are being "unfaithful" to the budget they both agreed to follow.

It's really easy to get caught up in the excitement and anticipation of your venture. Before you know it, your choices have snowballed into more than you planned. For example, Chris and Judy headed to the local construction center to pick out the items they wanted for a second bathroom they were adding to their home. They spent hours walking through the plumbing, bathroom, lighting and flooring departments looking at the options. It was exhilarating because they had been saving for years to add this bathroom. Slowly, they realized they were going over budget with their choice of items. They consciously and collectively decided to go $1500 over budget.

Again, the use of the term "financial infidelity" may give the impression one partner is deceiving the other partner. Not necessarily true. Chris and Judy mutually decided to go outside of their agreed upon budget.

So, is this an example of financial infidelity? Or not? Just because you mutually agree to expenses outside your budget doesn't mean it will turn out well.

Dale and Jennifer were building their fourth house. This time around, they were extra excited because they were building smaller and committed to staying within a strict budget. That, they said, was the whole point of building this home. They had learned the hard way that building big wasn't building better in their world. Dale and Jennifer had financially overbuilt three times before. They paid a high price each time with stress and strain caused by huge mortgages.

Fortunately they made money on their last house. It sold quickly and for a nice profit. They were relieved to get back into financial alignment. Paying off credit cards felt good. Now the plan was to buy an existing home financially within their means and to get financial professional guidance. Life was looking up for them.

They had decided to build again because they couldn't find a house that fit their values. With their renewed energy and lessons learned they thought building again would be ok. A lot went right for them in their decision-making process with this house. It was smaller and fewer frills were used. Then the credit card temptation reared its ugly head. Dale and Jennifer decided together it was ok to run up the cards because, even though they didn't want to, it felt necessary to get into their house they way they wanted it. They told themselves that this time they had done so much right it was ok to step out on their budget. They reminded each other that this was a joint decision, made for necessary purchases, and all would be ok. In the end, they once again had overwhelming and unnecessary consumer debt.

We're not saying you can't change things once your budget is in place. Be smart about it. Remember, your dreams, needs and values are the foundation of your project. The budget guides your choices and controls your costs. It is much wiser to revise your budget than disregard it.

As you evaluate choices and make decisions that go above and beyond your budget you could consider the following:

- Before making a decision, take a day or two to reevaluate. If, after a couple days, your choice(s) to alter your plans still seems like a good idea, then a revision may be in order.

- Consider the ripple affects of your decision. Example: Will it influence my loan? Will I have to let go of something else?

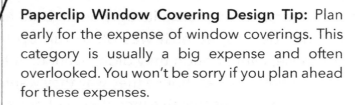

Paperclip Window Covering Design Tip: Plan early for the expense of window coverings. This category is usually a big expense and often overlooked. You won't be sorry if you plan ahead for these expenses.

One Last Thought

WARNING: Don't read this section unless you are willing to try something drastic! If you're not, it really is OK because what we are about to share with you is not for everyone.

Thinking something radical, feeling something radical or doing something radical is just what you need. For most people, what we are about to share sounds drastic, fanatical or possibly profound. Yet, it has helped millions of people all over the world! Open your mind, be willing to consider an unusual idea, and who knows what might happen?

Here it is.

What if everything you owned wasn't yours. What if the clothes on your back, the food you buy at the grocery store, the car you've made 60 payments on or the home you're about to build or remodel isn't yours. What if you don't own anything? Instead, you are the steward of all that you have.

Just like a manager oversees a restaurant or store, a bailiff supervises prisoners, or an estate manager oversees the whole of somebody's property, a steward manages someone else's household, property or finances.

Stewards are typically elected or chosen to these supervisory positions because they are trustworthy, faithful and wise. A good manager has succeeded in leading his employees and operating his business. A bailiff is selected to maintain order and safety in a courtroom and an estate manager is chosen to run an estate for someone. This may include property and household management duties such as:

- Cooking and/or gardening for the home or homes

- Hiring and directing other household staff

- Booking travel arrangements

- Maintaining household security

- Running errands

- Organizing and running large household events, parties, etc.

- Managing the household calendar

- Performing bookkeeping and/or accounting tasks

- Managing designated projects

These duties sound familiar? Most of you have the title of "estate manager" because you perform the above duties in your own home on a daily basis. Some are hired to carry out these duties for others.

A radical way to look at the money and possessions you currently have, and the money and the belongings you will acquire in the future, is as a gift. A gift from God. In ancient spiritual teachings and up-to-date biblical wisdom, God is the sole owner of everything.

Outstanding author, Larry Burkett observed, "When we acknowledge God's ownership, every spending decision becomes a spiritual decision. No longer do we ask, "God, what do You want me to do with *my* money?" The question is restated, "God, what do You want me to do with Your money?"

> *"It's good to have money and the things that money can buy, but it's good, too, to check up once in a while and make sure that you haven't lost the things that money can't buy."*
> ~George Horace Lorimer

When we have this perspective and, yes, it can feel radical, spending and saving decisions are equally as spiritual as giving decisions. If God is the owner and master of all things, our responsibility is to be good stewards. The position of a steward, manager, or bailiff is one of great responsibility, under the leadership of God. God has put us in charge of everything. He owns it, but we have the privilege of being the stewards of all he provides for us.

A friend of ours, Bill, and his father, Alan, shared the love of old cars. They appreciated buying worn out, rusty old cars and restoring them together. The last car they bought together sat in the garage for years as they just couldn't find the time to restore it. Alan's health began to deteriorate and he knew he and Bill would not get to work on their car together. Before Alan passed away, he gifted the car to Bill.

Bill was grateful to have the car. He wanted to take care of it and restore it one day in the honor of his father. Today, Bill has not finished restoring the car but has been a reliable and responsible steward. As he works on restoring the car, he remembers the good times he had with his father.

Do you remember the last time you were given a gift that had deep meaning and significance to you? I bet you really wanted to take care of it! What if you approached life, money and other resources with that kind of reverence? All we have is a gift and our role is to be a wise steward.

Money is one of many resources available to you. Use it wisely. More importantly, your relationship, family and friends are more valuable. Live in integrity.

Reflection Questions

In addition to the previous activities in this chapter, here are a few questions you can think through and share with your spouse:

1. Is there any part of the project that just doesn't feel right? Why?
    Examples: Are we spending too much money? Are we holding back from anything?

2. What does God want us to do?
    Examples: Listen? Stop? Do we wait or go for it? Ask for help?

3. How can we be a good steward with what has been given to us?
    Examples: Do our goals align with our needs and values?

"To expect the unexpected shows a thoroughly modern intellect."

~Oscar Wilde

 **Key Six:**

Expect the Unexpected

WE'VE NEVER HEARD OF A REMODELING or building project that has gone perfectly according to plan. Have you? Probably not. Unfortunately, life rarely flows seamlessly without a hiccup here or there. While planning is vital to a successful completion, you will do yourself an enormous favor if you assume that at least one, and most likely more than one, unexpected delays, detours or unwanted surprises will occur during the process.

Detours

Building a new home and doing major remodeling projects are big tasks. Once into the project, new ideas may arise, requiring a bit more time to research their viability. This is more common than you might think. Detours need to be anticipated. Projects like this take on a life of their own and that's part of the fun.

When Mark and Laura were in the framing process of building their home, they saw an opportunity to incorporate a unique window into their kitchen. This wasn't in the original blueprint, but the more they talked about this window the more excited they became, as this additional window would add more light and character to the kitchen.

Both Mark and Laura realized they could get diverted away from the original building plan by adding this window. Their builder helped them assess the pros and cons of adding this window from a cost and timing perspective. They looked at:

- Was the cost of the window an additional expense they were willing to take on? Could they afford it?

- Would adding the window impact the timing of the building project? Would the addition of this window put them behind?

Mark and Laura determined they could add the additional cost of the window to the overall budget because it was a change they both really desired. Including the window in their kitchen allowed more natural light and charm to the kitchen. Ordering the window did set back the completion of the overall window installment for the home. Fortunately, it didn't impact the overall home construction completion date.

Paperclip Counter Top Installation Tip:
Installation of countertops is one of the last tasks to be finished to complete your home construction. Be aware that some loans cannot be closed without installed counter surfaces. The template has to be made after the cabinets are installed. If you are using granite, quartz or other solid surfaces, it can take awhile to be fabricated.

Another couple, Rick and Julie had the option of adding more room to the entryway of their existing home. The builder shared an idea of increasing the walkway area that added esthetic value and functional purpose. However, as they discussed this, they realized the area would gather a lot of snow in the wintertime. The sun would not reach this area so the snow would not melt. This would allow for a snow and ice build-up.

Rick had back problems and couldn't shovel the significant amount of snow that would accumulate, and Julie couldn't help out with the snow removal either. So, Rick, Julie and the builder researched the cost of adding heat to the concrete so the snow and ice could melt off. The research indicated it would be too costly for them to add the in-concrete heating. They decided not to add the additional area to their entry way and, in the end, were happy with this decision.

These simple examples of getting "detoured" in your building project can be a regular occurrence while building or remodeling. Problems or opportunities can interrupt your process and be overwhelming, especially if unanticipated problems shout for your attention. It is useful to consider the previous questions to determine if your choice will help you stay focused or take you down a road you may or may not want to take. Mark and Laura decided to take the detour of adding a window and Rick and Julie determined it wasn't in their best interest to add the walkway.

Most of you will need to continue working and take care of your families as you build or remodel. Your everyday life responsibilities will need to be tended to as you're completing your project. You can quickly get consumed with your construction project and before you know it home, work and family obligations are piling up. You may have so much enthusiasm and focus on your new project that the mundane, everyday duties get ignored.

Maybe you're sick of your project already? Maybe you've been working weeks and months without a break? It's easy to do because there are deadlines to keep with projected completions dates. It can all be so overwhelming! *Ugh!*

Paperclip Deadline Tip: Deadlines are deadly in decorating. Your contractor and designer will cringe if they hear you say "We have to be in by Christmas!" That is a setup for disappointment and frustration for all concerned. To stay at peace, manage your timing expectations.

Unexpected Building Disasters

The story we are about to share is really hard to believe because so many truly unexpected and unlikely things went wrong with the remodel of a bathroom. But it is a very real story. What is more amazing is how Tony and Diana dealt with the stress of it all.

Our story starts when the bathroom remodel's completion date was less than four months away. They had this goal because their house would be full of guests for an upcoming event. Everything was moving smoothly until one, significant mistake was made, which started a ripple effect of mishaps.

What was the fateful mistake? The measurement of the quartz countertop was off. This was discovered when the installers arrived with one that was a bit too big. The installers of the countertop tried to make it fit and the countertop broke in half. When it broke, a sidewall was gouged and the sheetrock was scraped. The wall had to be repaired and a new slab had to be ordered which delayed the countertop installation by a week.

One week turned to three when they got a call from the electrician who had been bitten by a spider and had to be hospitalized. This put the project further behind.

One of Tony and Diana's relatives passed away unexpectedly, and they left for a week to be with the family. Sandy kept the project going, but was unable to get in touch with them for most of this time, delaying the project further.

The family had made vacation plans on the basis of the bathroom being finished according to schedule. Unable to get a refund, Tony and Diana went ahead with the vacation. While they were away, the shower was finished. That was good news.

But there was a small problem with a valve located inside the wall behind the shower. The plumber's assistant tried to move it, which required a blowtorch. Unluckily, the backer board caught on fire, inside the wall itself. By the time the fire was put out, the wall was compromised. As a consequence, the entire shower had to be redone. It is still unsure if the plumber's insurance will pay for the mistake and there may be a lawsuit.

The shower re-do required the tile to be reset. However, the stress mounted as it was discovered that the tile setter, having already finished the shower once, was about to leave on a three-week vacation in two days. The tile setter worked himself to exhaustion, but finished the job before he left on his vacation. It was impossible to get the glass shower door installed before he left, so he went to a local store, bought a shower curtain and rod, installed that so at least the home owners could use their shower. Upon his return, he was already committed to another job, so he had to re-do the project in record time. Fortunately, this did not delay the project much.

Lastly, the glass company who was producing the mirrors said they didn't have enough chrome sleutter in stock. For that reason, they had to order the chrome and it took two additional weeks to get in. More delays!

Tony and Diana are good at dealing with stress. They aren't perfect at it, but they have amazing and effective skills to handle what life throws at them. In the **How to Deal With the Unexpected Makes a Difference** section we summarized their approach, attitude and ability in dealing with the many unexpected events that happened throughout their remodel escapade.

Losses Prior to Beginning the Build

Life can be unpredictable. Stuff happens. Crap happens. S*** happens. Life and death happens.

After twenty-five years of visualizing their dream home, Mark and Laura broke ground. Unfortunately, they did so with much trepidation due to three significant deaths in their family in one year. The sense of adventure and enthusiasm was darkened by deep sorrow and pain. Both Mark and Laura knew building a home would be stressful. They knew a relationship that wasn't strained by major life issues would be stretched and challenged under home construction.

When they combined the significant losses they had just experienced together with the added stress of building, they were not sure it was the right time to do anything, let alone build a house.

They discussed the timing of the housing market, the life stage of their family, and the grief the family was going through at the time. The finances to build the home were there and the costs to build the home were average. Though unexpected, the inheritance they received meant they were able to spend more on building than they had previously planned, easing some financial concerns.

Their new property was very close to their old home, so the move would not impact their two teenage children. The teenagers were very excited about designing and decorating their own rooms and living in a new home. How thrilling for them!

"It's good to have money and the things that money can buy, but it's good, too, to check up once in a while and make sure that you haven't lost the things that money can't buy."
~George Horace Lorimer

Mark and Laura were very conscious of the grief they were both experiencing. Further, Laura wasn't sure she even wanted to build a house because she had watched friends and family build homes and it was very hard on their relationships. Laura and Mark had difficulties communicating in their relationship and she thought building would push them over the edge. She knew their grief would be added on to the normal stress; she didn't want to move ahead.

Mark on the other hand was very excited about building as he found the perfect piece of property and envisioned his dream home there. He was ready to have a project to work on in the midst of his grief. The building project would help him to have something else to focus on besides the deep sadness he was feeling. Even though he agreed with Laura that home building was stressful, Mark was ready to go.

They each had their own individual answers to "Is it the right time to build, or not"? Laura definitely believed it was not the right time to build. Mark was passionate about it and was excited things were falling into place. As they discussed the situation more, there were several points that helped them make a decision to build at that time.

First, Laura wanted to support Mark because he was so motivated and enthusiastic. Second, they knew the builder very well and he had inside knowledge of the family situation. They all went into the project with eyes wide open. Lastly, Laura meditated and prayed on the blessing of inheritance and how her mother would be overjoyed knowing how much she helped her and Mark build the house of their dreams. Laura made a conscience choice to be soothed by her mother's loving memory and gift when the stress crept into her marriage.

The home they built together was beautiful, and they enjoy it very much. And yet, it is reasonable to wonder whether waiting a year would have been less stressful. Was it wise for them to express their grief through the building process, or could there have been a better route to take? We don't know the answer. But it is important if you find yourself in a similar situation to look at your course of action from different perspectives before continuing with a planned build or remodel. It's okay to change the timing of your project.

Life Trauma During the Build

Another couple were in the middle of a remodel when tragedy struck their family. Ami and Nate needed to finish the landscaping after a major remodel/addition to their house. They had been living with tarp on the would-be lawn for over a year.

Sadly, Nathan's brother died in the month of April, the month they were due to start the landscaping project. Nathan was numb and devastated by the loss of his brother. Yet, along with the shocking death came an inheritance check from his brother's life insurance policy. This unexpected extra money would help them complete more of their landscaping goals.

Nate anticipated the landscaping project would be therapeutic for him, especially when he decided to make a memorial to his brother. But the process wasn't as healing as he'd hoped. He became obsessed with making sure the memorial was "just right." Before long, he became overwhelmed, distraught and quick to anger. He was trying to work through his emotions with this project, but paid the price through too much pain in his body and his checkbook.

Despite the physical and emotional pain, the end result of the landscaping was absolutely beautiful: a rock memorial, a waterfall and pond, a fire pit and many lovely shrubs and trees. His family and friends could enjoy the new backyard and warmly remember their son, brother and friend.

In spite of the positive outcome, was it too close to Nate's brother's death to make a clear, conscious effort to honor his brother the way he did? Might he have saved himself additional emotional distress and kept from herniating a disc if the project had been postponed a few months or years?

If you find yourself in the midst of grief and loss it would be helpful to assess if it's the right time for you to build or remodel. Choosing wisely can be the difference between a disaster and a positive, memorable experience.

Unexpected Good News

Tony and Maggie are a young couple in their twenties. They had been happily married for four years and were eager to start a family. They knew they would not be able to birth their own child and wanted to offer children a home by being foster parents. Ultimately, their hope was that it could lead to adoption.

They worked with a social services agency and knew God had the perfect child to add to their family. They weren't sure when a child would come into their life. They had been waiting patiently a little over a year when they found the perfect starter home.

A new planned community going up close to Tony's work had all the features they were looking for in a neighborhood, with a church, a new mall and close access to a few lakes. Being part of a church family was important to them. Maggie was hoping to work part time in retail, so the mall could offer her employment that was close to home. Both Tony and Maggie loved the outdoors. They liked to fish, bike, swim and water ski. This location was exactly what they were looking for as they dreamed of a new home.

Tony and Maggie were jazzed when they were able to somewhat customize their new, two bedroom home. They picked out the cabinets they liked, the kitchen and bathroom counter tops, the paint colors and carpeting that reflected their family. It was all they dreamed it would be.

Then the week they were moving into their new home they got a call from the social service agency stating they had an eight year old girl named Pearl they would like to place in their home. What an exciting week, moving into a new home and having the possibility of adding to their family.

The move and adjustment of a child coming into their home was sudden and a bit overwhelming. Pearl had been living in chaos for much of her life so Tony and Maggie didn't want to add to it. They wanted to create a safe and stable environment for her. While they wanted to bring Pearl into their home immediately, they knew it was best for all of them if they waited a week or so.

Amazingly, Pearl came to live with Tony and Maggie ten days after they moved into their new home. They were able to provide a stable and safe home for Pearl, something she had not experienced before. Because they had just moved into the home, Pearl's room was not fully decorated so Maggie used this as an opportunity to allow Pearl to create her own space. What a special time for all of them!

In the end, Pearl stayed with Tony and Maggie as a foster child for over two years and eventually became their adopted daughter.

This is an uplifting example of an unexpected change happening during a building project. While this didn't happen in the midst of the actual building phase, it significantly impacted Tony and Maggie's life long-term. They had been somewhat preparing themselves for an addition to their family, yet were taken off guard by the timing. They were wise in stepping back to assess the situation and make a decision that benefited all of them.

Spiritual Strength

Many people talk about how their spiritual life impacts their decision making process. They take their ideas, thoughts, dreams and decisions to a power greater than themselves. Some people call this a higher power or God.

Mark and Laura believed God had blessed them with the money to build their dream home. They wanted to honor their deceased family members and God with using the money wisely. For them, they prayed for God's wisdom on whether or not they should build the home and if it was the right time. They were willing to let go of their agenda and desire to do what God wanted them to do.

Mike and Neda built most of their home with their own hands. They worked hard through rain and snow. Sometimes Mother Nature pushed them behind schedule. Consequently, they worked harder in the weeks to come. Eventually they were exhausted, impatient and grouchy and had very little time for their children

After much prayer and consideration regarding the emotional state of the family, Mike and Neda decided to take Sunday's off from anything to do with building the house. They attended church, spent time with their kids and friends, and made every effort to have fun and relax.

Doing this actually improved the overall morale, attitude and physical well being of the whole family. In addition, they completed the house on time as planned.

In both of these stories, their greatest desire was to know what God wanted for them. How to be the best stewards of what God had given them. So prayer can be a powerful tool for guidance and help keep the relationship grounded and healthy.

The previous stories illustrate that life is very full— full of happiness, opportunities and the unexpected. The challenge we face throughout our lives is how we are going to respond to it. It is wise to take the time to assess and ask if this is the right time. If it is, how do you move forward? If it's not, wait. If life gives you a surprise and you're forced to deal with the unforeseen, seek out the support and help of professionals, family and friends, and God.

How We Deal with the Unexpected that Makes the Difference

These stories we've shared feel a bit sad, dismal or overwhelming. Life is full of the unexpected, full of pain *and* joy. No one expected such heartbreak. You, too, may have experienced many surprises in life. You can't control what is going to take place as you try to plan and predict what will happen tomorrow, next month or ten years from now.

How you deal with the unknown that crashes into your life makes a difference. If you find yourself in the middle of abrupt change, here are a few suggestions to help you through.

- Be kind to yourself and others around you as you adjust to the change. It takes time to adapt to what has happened. You may feel a little "foggy" or out of sorts; it's normal.

- Allow yourself to feel. Feel all of what is going on. Stuffing or ignoring your emotions won't help. In the long run, it will only harm you.

- Take a break from your building project if needed.

- Seek help and support from family, friends and professionals. They may be able to hear and see things from a different perspective. They can help you through the change and your building project.

In the next chapter, we are going to offer specific ways to deal with unexpected crises and the stress inherent in a building or remodeling project. But we have provided reflection questions in this chapter to help you think through how you can handle the unexpected joys and losses life may throw your way.

Reflection Questions

Here is a summary of questions you can ask yourself when considering if this is the "right time." In addition, please reflect on the thoughts provided earlier in the chapter.

1. Consider all factors that will be impacted by your decision to build or remodel

   - Family, work, location, resources

2. How will this influence your other life goals?

3. Have you prayed about this?

We encourage you to take the time to talk with your spouse about the answers to these questions so you can be prepared for the task at hand.

"In times of stress, the best thing we can do for each other is to listen with our ears and our hearts and to be assured that our questions are just as important as our answers."

~Fred Rogers, *The World According to Mister Rogers: Important Things to Remember*

 **Key Seven:**

Survive the Stress

YOU KNOW STRESS. THAT FEELING OF BEING anxious, overwhelmed, and tired. You may even know it intimately if you are full of stress on a daily basis. For others, you have chosen to deal with the challenges that come your way with minimal stress. Our lives do not come challenge free or stress free.

If you asked ten people what stress is, what causes stress or how stress feels, you would most likely get ten different answers. People define, experience and deal with stress differently. Stress is difficult to define for scientists, let alone the average person, because it's a subjective phenomenon for each of us. The American Institute of Stress describes over fifty different signs and symptoms of stress. At the top of the list, people physically experience stress by frequent headaches, jaw clenching or pain to name a few.

Stress can have extensive power that impact emotions, mood and behavior. Equally important but often less appreciated are effects on various systems in the body, organs and tissues throughout your body. It impacts your nervous, musculoskeletal, cardiovascular, reproductive, endocrine, respiratory and gastrointestinal systems. That just about covers all of your body and mind. Ouch!

In the midst of your construction project you may feel confused, overwhelmed, anxious, tired or depressed. You may have trouble problem solving and your coping skills may have "left the building." You could experience headaches, stomachaches, increased heart rate and other physical manifestations of stress. In fact, general physicians state that 70% of all office visits are stress related.

We as humans are very creative with the ways we try to deal with stress. Unfortunately, we frequently see in the media the impact of unhealthy coping behaviors. Over consumption of alcohol, street drugs and prescription medications, eating too much or not enough, gambling or overspending, obsessed with sex or avoiding it, to name a few. The list could go on and on.

For most of you, remodeling or building your home will be challenging. As you read in the last chapter, unexpected things happen to people, things that are out of your control. Stuff happens! Don't' let this get you down or discouraged.

Paperclip Glass Shower Door Design Tip: If you are having a glass shower door, especially a steam shower door, know that it is usually one of the last installations done in your new construction, other than window treatments. A shower needs to be measured for a door after the entire tile around the door is totally done. It can take two weeks or more for the door company to get that shower door installed. By this time, you're pretty excited to get in that shower, so this seems to take forever. Maybe bribing the door company with cookies (or beer) will help speed things along, but I doubt it! If you had a natural stone or marble tile done in your shower, you will need to not use it for two weeks anyway to let the tile and grout sealer do its thing.

Stress is complex and can also have a positive impact. There is positive stress. Athletes have stress levels motivationally high for peak performance, but not too high. Moms, executives and workers handle stress like a rubber band. They have learned to stretch with commitment and challenge but not be overwhelmed or snap. The solution is to know the perimeter of your stress, where it is motivating you, and the limits to where you won't break.

How you respond to stress is key. Just like stress differs for you, stress management is also unique to you. How you cope with stress is most likely different from how your spouse or your general contractor deals with it.

Focus on What You Can Control

Tony and Diana were able to determine those things they could and could not control. For example, they realized they could have been more efficient in the beginning by doing more research on what types of products they wanted to use in their remodel. They learned from their mistakes. They also made a conscious effort not to fret over what they couldn't change.

> *"Pessimism leads to weakness, optimism to power".*
> ~William James

Change Your Thinking

The American Institute of Stress state in their research that life is full of stressful events. They apply the 90/10 rule. Ten percent of your life is what happens to you and ninety percent is how you respond to it. Unexpected things happen and it's your response that determines the level of stress you experience.

Tony and Dianna chose to deal with what was in front of them. They live with the mindset of simplicity. Think basic, do what is in front of you and move step by step. Life doesn't have to be complicated.

If you've ever had a problem playing golf or other sports, most of the time you go back to the basics. In golf, you might go back and assess your grip or swing. Evaluate your stance, the position of your head or shoulders, and the location of your club in relationship to the ball. You assess one element at a time. This gives a sense of accomplishment and provides direction for the next steps.

One more idea to help to change your thinking to something more productive is to notice where your attention goes. Is it focusing on negative thoughts or finding resolution? Tony could have ruminated on thoughts like "Why does this always happen to me? Nothing ever goes my way. Those people are such idiots." He could have gotten trapped in this line of thinking. But he didn't.

Maybe you get stuck in thoughts like this? Wherever you put your attention, it grows. You can change your thinking by changing what you focus on.

Change your Attitude

"Is the glass half full or half empty?" Tony and Dianna both look at life with a "half full" and a "can do" attitude. Even though they were upset about the mistakes made, they chose to deal with the events from a positive, empowering outlook and perspective.

Tony and Dianna know that change is inevitable! Remind yourself of this during your project. How you choose to deal with change can influence your level of stress. We aren't recommending you pooh pooh or diminish a mistake, avoid conflict or stick your head in the sand. It's ok to be upset, mad, angry, anxious or fearful. When something goes wrong, it's OK to be upset. Challenges will always be out there and your attitude and thoughts are the key holders to the stress you experience.

To summarize:

- Determine what is in your control

- Reframe your thinking

- Change your attitude and redirect your attention

Take a Break

Maybe it's time for a break! People get tired of their whole life revolving around the new house or remodel job. Or sometimes it's just feeling overwhelmed with having to make so many decisions. It's OK to take time off. It can help you feel refreshed and rekindle the enthusiasm you had at the start of your project.

> "The basic building block of good communications is the feeling that every human being is unique and of value."
> ~Unknown

Perhaps you've been building your house for years. Maybe you're doing the remodel job yourself when you have the time and money. Predictably, it's taking way longer than you thought it would. The dedication and passion have crumbled.

Many times relationships lose passion and become stagnate or boring. Projects can feel like that, too. Here are a couple ideas that can kick-start your relationship and desire to move toward your goal.

- Ask for help from your friends. This could help you get done faster and have fun, too.

- Get professional help. Hire someone to complete a part of the project you don't want to do or don't feel qualified to do.

- Know what excites you, jazzes you and keeps you motivated. See Key 3 to dive into this subject more. When you know what that is, do it! Having some energy about the project keeps you inspired and determined.

We want you to know it is natural to get sidetracked. So don't be surprised when it happens because it's not a

> *"A couple's relationship will be remodeled along with their home."*
> ~Laura Longville

question of "will it happen" but more of "when will it happen." Be prepared for when it happens and realize you're normal and you can get unstuck!

Communicate in a Positive Way

Challenges come in all forms. Some stress we create by the choices we make (lying about finances) and others times, life just happens (measuring mistakes, illness, death, etc.). In addition, sometimes the way we communicate instigates stress.

The most significant truth we've discovered is that *a couple's relationship will be remodeled along with their home.* Often times it's the way we communicate or don't communicate that causes the problem.

Dr.'s John and Julie Gottman of the Gottman Institute are experts in the field of marriage counseling. They have done over thirty-five years of research on what works and doesn't work in a committed relationship. We aren't going to be able to cover all of their advice in this book, but will share with you their top communication tools to incorporate in your relationship. I would highly recommend you read any of their books or attend their seminars. It will make you a better partner in your relationship and help your marriage flourish.

Tom and Nancy are a fun loving couple. He is robust, friendly with a big smile and Nancy is feisty in a goodhearted way and always bubbly. They love to golf and play cards. Tom loves music, especially the English rock bands of the '60's. Nancy loves her children and grandchildren from a previous marriage and didn't work outside the home. Sandy worked for them on several different occasions and this time was hired to help them build their retirement home on a golf course.

Tom was present for a lot of the interior design choices because Nancy and Sandy asked him to be available for input and feedback. Sandy really wanted to get a sense of how she could best incorporate his personality in their home. However, when he did give his opinion and desires and it didn't match Nancy's preference, she would almost always say, "He doesn't know anything."

Poor guy; he heard that so many times. Maybe he didn't really hear it at all, I don't know. Every time I heard Nancy say that, I would cringe and hold my breath and expect a protest from him. However, he never appeared to have a reaction to being put in the category of not knowing anything.

> "Every couple needs to argue now and then. Just to prove that the relationship is strong enough to survive. Long-term relationships, the ones that matter, are all about weathering the peaks and the valleys."
> ~Nicholas Sparks

Obviously to attain his level of professional success, he did know a lot. Regardless, on the home front, "he didn't know anything" unless his opinion matched Nancy's vision. So many times when couples build or remodel, the husband or male partner is in the background when it comes to the interior design choices. There are a lot of decisions to be made: themes, color choices, styles, and preferences on room functions, to name a few. Verbally, the wives we work with state they want their husbands to be involved, but do they really? The jury is still out in this case.

This is one example of what can stifle and even hinder open communication in a relationship. This real life situation is as complex as most relationships are. People say and do things that make perfect sense to them at the time.

There are four ways that you can shut down communication.

- Be Critical: Being critical attacks your partner's personality or character, usually with the intent of making you right and them wrong: "He doesn't know anything."

- Be Defensive: Being defensive shows up when you make excuses, disagree and/or cross complain or avoid any responsibility.

- Show Contempt: Showing contempt comes with name-calling and demeaning comments. It includes eye rolling, sneering and curling your lip.

- Stonewall: Stonewalling is a way to avoid conflict. It includes the silent treatment, withdrawing from one another, removing yourself physically or changing the subject.

You may be in relationships that are challenging even prior to your construction project. You may even think to yourself "I really am worried about what our building project is going to do to our marriage." Maybe you've even wondered why you're still in your relationship? Don't lose hope.

We do have a few simple skills you can use to help your communication flow easier in the midst of your stress. When you're exhausted and overwhelmed with your construction demands and life responsibilities, use one or two of the suggestions below or things you may have learned in other parts of this book. The point is, recognize your part in what isn't going well and then make a change.

Paperclip Electrical Design Tip 1: If you want electric power in the floor of the basement, don't miss your golden opportunity to show where you want them before the concrete is poured! It's easy to miss this window. You, your contractor, project manager, or your interior designer, or someone needs to communicate this to the electrician and concrete company.

Seven Simple Ways to Strengthen Your Relationships

1. Slow down, take a break, ask for help.

2. Be respectful and honest in love. Respect can go a long way. It can soothe the sting of a hurtful comment and redirect the conversation to something more productive. From the previous story, Tom might have said something like "I wish I knew something about interior design. I do have some ideas that I would like you to consider. Do you think we could work together with Sandy on this?"

3. Turn a complaint into a request.

4. Validate your partner. "I know you are tired. Is there anything I can do to help?", "You sound frustrated, what can I do?" Let them know you understand what they are experiencing and that you care.

5. Claim responsibility. "What is my part?", "What can I do?"

6. Shift to appreciations with one another. Shower each with gratitude and thanks. For example, "Thanks for all the hard work you do to keep the house running", "You handled the contractor really well today when the conversation got a little heated."

7. Repeat.

Changing how you communicate takes effort and commitment. You have a familiar way of communicating that works and doesn't work. It's your default mode of operation. We know it's hard to make a change and it's worth the energy and dedication!

Henry and Mary Lou are great examples for all of us. They are an older couple that incorporates many of these tools in their marriage. Sandy was part of several projects with them to include new carpet and tile floor installation, updated countertops, changed paint colors, draperies, and helped buy and arrange new furniture. The sweet words of encouragement they had for one another carried them through many stressful situations.

They were tender in sharing their gratitude and were always respectful with each other. True role models.

Make all the decisions as a team. Be in sync and make it fun. Marriage and close relationships require purposeful attention. Don't let the stress of your construction goals deter your love and commitment to one another. Remember. . . your relationship is more important than anything else!

Home Building and Remodeling are challenging. How you handle these challenges will determine how much stress you experience. Review the suggestions throughout this chapter to help you cope with the trials you encounter. The questions provide additional opportunities for you to talk with your spouse about stress.

Reflection Questions

1. How do I experience stress? (i.e.; headaches, fear, tired, try harder . . .)

2. What are the situations that create stress for me?

3. What can I do to prepare ahead of time to relieve or reduce the stress? How can I take care of myself? (i.e. get good sleep, eat well, exercise, make time for my spouse and kids, have fun, etc.)

4. List your resources you can call when stressed out. (i.e. family, friends, counselor, Dr., etc.)

"For every evil under the sun, there
is a remedy, or there is none.
"If there be, try and find it. If there
is none, never mind it".

~Mother Goose Rhymes,
Mother Goose Rhy Color

PART 2

Tools of the Trade

YOU'RE ALMOST TO THE END OF THIS BOOK. WE hope you are energized and motivated about your building project. You have been dreaming big and visualizing all that you want to include in your dream home. You are more aware of why this project is so important to you AND that your values and needs are driving your ideas. In addition, your blueprint or some kind of guidance mechanism is vital to your success.

This section is about giving you a lot of helpful tools and highly recommended resources to make you as successful as possible. In fact, you might even have jumped ahead to this section to get your project going. If you are a reader who likes to jump around in a book and read bits and pieces, we would recommend you go back to the previous chapters and actually read them in order. We think it will give you a well-rounded perspective of taking on a remodel job or home building adventure.

Quick Reference Checklist

Keep this list handy as you move through the building process. In addition, your builder will provide more detail in each step.

- Hiring a General Contractor

- Grading and site preparation

- Constructing Foundation

- Framing

- Installation of windows and doors

- Roofing

- Siding

- Rough Electrical

- Rough Plumbing

- Rough heating, air conditioning, furnace (HVAC)

- Drywall – sheetrock, tape and texture

- Underlayment or sub floor

- Trimming doors and molding around doors, windows and base boards

- Painting

- Finish Electrical

- Bathroom and kitchen counters and cabinets

- Finish Plumbing

- Install floor coverings

- Finish HVAC

- Punch List – The builder inspects the house. All concerns are listed. The various contractors return to fix the problems.

How to Hire a General Contractor

We strongly recommend you interview several general contractors (GC's). Building a dream home or any significant remodel job is worth spending a significant amount of time interviewing GC's to make sure the fit is right. Just like in any other profession, you want to make sure your GC will work with you and for you. In the same way that it's important finding the right Obstetrician when you're having a baby, hiring the best defense attorney when you've been wrongly accused, or going to the best Oncologist if you have cancer, hiring the right GC may be the difference between having a good experience building a home and an awful one.

Questions to Ask a General Contractor

1. What motivates you to do excellent work?

2. What are your strengths? What are your weaknesses?

3. Are you licensed – bonded – insured?

4. How long have you been in business?

5. Do you do your own work or use all or some subcontractors?

6. Are there possible reasons you would not be regularly on the job?

7. Can you give us references?

8. How do you market your business?

9. What career related organizations do you belong to?

10. What is your employment history?

11. How do you handle mistakes and disagreements? Tell us about a time you had a problem with a subcontractor.

12. Which of these best describe your work style? Are you creative, structured, organized, tidy, big-picture, detailed, or a team player to name a few.?

13. If something was to happen to you and you weren't able to complete your GC obligations, what is your back up plan? Who will fulfill those responsibilities?

14. Based on our loan amount, will we be given a detailed budget from which to work? How much a square foot will our project cost?

15. What happens when we change our mind about a few things during construction? How do you handle change orders?

16. What purchases will we be responsible for? Where do you prefer us to shop?

17. If we have communication problems, conflict or tension between us as a couple, how can you help us? What relationship skills do you have that could help us?

18. Can we depend on you to help us determine our time line? We need a contractor who will help us develop the plans, sections, elevations, door and finish schedules, fully developed windows, as well as a full set of specifications. We will allow plenty of time for this, but we need consistent effort from you. Does that work for you?

We highly recommend both of you interview the general contractor together. It is important you both agree that you can work with the GC you have chosen. Discuss if you get the sense or a feeling that you may not be able to create and maintain a good working relationship with this contractor. This is a step worth taking some time on. If you don't find the suitable person right away, don't be discouraged. Keep looking and wait for the perfect fit for you.

Paperclip Wall Texture Design Tip: Choosing your wall texture is often overlooked until the time is NOW to decide, while the texture guys are staring at you. Know the terminology they use. There is orange peel, light knock down, medium knock down, heavy knockdown, troweled mud to name a few. Start to notice walls as you move through your day and when you see something you like, find out what texture is called. Make sure the texture crew does a sample board for you from scrap sheetrock there on the job. If you want no texture, be prepared to pay the painter more, as smooth walls are hard to paint. They tend to show all the little imperfections and paint strokes.

What a General Contractor Wants You to Know

On the other side of the homebuilder coin is the General Contractor. In respect, the GC will be interviewing you as well to make sure working with you is a good fit for him or her. We asked a couple General Contractors about the building process and here are their responses. It can help you see the importance of having good workable relationship with one another:

1. What motivates you to do excellent work?

GC 1: I want to feel proud of the work we do. It feels good when our company is acknowledged for doing excellent work and doing the right thing. I want to build long term relationships with our clients. We depend on our reputation to move our company forward. Money is how you keep score, but excellent work is to be expected regardless of the money.

GC 2: Integrity and organization skills are a learned behavior and are central to an effective general contractor. Being adequately paid for my expertise should provide a quality experience, on time and on budget. Commitment to quality is setting the bar for the sub-contractors to make money and have a positive experience.

2. In, general, a lot of people do not trust general contractors. Why do you think that is?

GC 1: They should trust GC's because we are professionals. Having said that, like a lot of professions, the fifteen or so percent of bad apples makes it hard for the rest of us who are trustworthy pros at what we do. Some people call themselves general contractors and they are not. This happens more in the residential market than commercial work. Some contractors tell you what you want to hear and promise more than they can deliver. Check out a GC by getting references. A word of mouth referral can help ease some concerns.

GC 2: Sometimes a GC doesn't do a good job. He may not have the experience or skill to do the job right. A skilled GC will glean out the project definition (the clients' wishes) up front, then interpolating that back into the project definition into an accurate and realistic budget. If their GC is chosen due to a popularity contest, the outcome is usually always negative. Popular GC's are typically ineffective schmoozers that don't know their business well enough to be leaders.

Sometimes the GC gets a bad rap because the homebuilder doesn't know what they want; they have difficulty making decisions or can't communicate effectively. Sometimes all three! Here are a few suggestions I have that help a GC do his job proficiently.

- Determine an agreed upon budget and stick to it. At the end of the day the project is always about the money, so the project must then be defined under the leadership of the GC as either a A. Firm Price B. A Cost Not To Exceed C. Or At Cost plus A Multiplier.

- Typically, the client is too emotionally invested in their project to trust the general contractor with their emotions. Their emotions have taken on a financial component that they have not defined up front. Therefore, until the emotional financial component has achieved balance or consensus, the GC will be the recipient of the negative because the client has failed to achieve consensus. It becomes much easier for the client to blame the GC for their financial emotional problems than it does for the client to blame their inability to communicate honestly or completely with themselves or their partner. The project does not hold the same emotional value to the GC as it holds with the client. A highly skilled GC has the ability to negotiate through the emotional intensity that can arise.

> *"A truly happy person is one who can enjoy the scenery on a detour".*
> ~Unknown

3. What is the definition of a General Contractor?

An educated, experienced person who assumes the risks involved in the construction of your home. He or she accepts responsibility for sole procurement of the total construction project. This includes, but is not limited to, the costs, budget, schedule and safety on the job. He is in charge of the skilled sub-contractors and craftspeople, holding them accountable for their work. There are benefits to hiring a GC who is an engineer. There are benefits in hiring a contractor who is involved in civic organizations and professional organizations like AGC-American Association of General Contractors. Good communication skills are paramount.

4. What questions are you, as the GC, typically asked during an interview to build a dream home?

Right off the bat, we are asked what we charge. We are asked about our experience and availability. We are asked how the budgeting process works, how the process works and where to begin.

5. What questions does a GC ask before accepting a job to build a dream home?

- What are your projected start and end dates? What is our schedule?

- Is this your first building project?

- What is your budget? Does your budget include the lot?

- What is the size of your lot?

- Do you see this as a short term or long term project? In other words, do you want to do the building in phases over time or all at once?

- What do you want to build? What is your vision?

- How involved do you want to be?

- Why did you choose our company as a possible choice to build your home?

6. **How much per square foot does it cost this year (2013) to build/remodel a home? Break it down into price points.**

   This is difficult to answer because it is based on so many factors, such as the level of finishes and design, location and product used.

   - A starter house with 1400 square feet main level with finished basement on 3/10 acre with a two-car garage is about $85.00 a square foot.

   - The same square footage home with semi-custom

choices is $120-$160/ square foot.

- Offering upper-end choices is about $180/square foot.

- At $270 per square foot, the sky may be the limit on choices.

- In general, the more complicated the project, the more expensive it is.

7. How much over budget (percentage) is typical?

A 5% over-run is typical on a project. To avoid this, study and research your project. Listen to your contractor. I must emphasize the importance of proper planning on the front end. Make timely decisions and don't emotionally fool yourselves about your choices and decisions.

8. How do you handle change orders?

GC 1: There are misconceptions about what a change order is. It's almost considered a bad word. The change orders should be homeowner driven. For instance, the homeowner does a walk through and determines they want a wall changed, not the contractor. The desire is listed on a change order form and the homeowner is charged for that. A change order generated by the contractor should not cost the homeowner any money. You should never hear "you owe me more money" because the contractor needs to make a construction change.

GC 2: Change orders usually start with a verbal agreement but they should always end up being documented: a note to files, an email, and a signed written change order, etc. As time goes on the changes build up and the cost goes up accordingly. As the cost goes up, the client usually finds themselves over budget, out of time and then they don't have the money to complete the project. As the project wraps up, the little things become the big issues between all parties. The client is upset their project ran out of money, did not get finished on time, or was not what they envisioned either originally or what it has now morphed into.

> *"More people would learn from their mistakes if they weren't so busy denying them."*
> ~Harold J. Smith.

The client cannot or will not be angry with themselves because in their minds they have always relied on the GC to control their budget, even if they made the conscious decision to go over their own budget, or that their project is late and is not being delivered on time. If every change order is not put into the perspective of its effect on the original budget, the original budget holds no merit and the project should have been handled with an open checkbook.

9. What drives you, the GC, crazy about building a client's dream home?

GC 1: We struggle with their lack of knowledge of the construction process. The inability to make decisions is huge! Trying to keep them objective when they tend to get too emotionally attached during the process can be stressful. They are usually new to all of this, especially the budget as it relates to their selections of products needed for the project. The sticker shock process is hard sometimes.

GC 2: The client who is an emotional based decision maker, who has no ability to relate their decisions to some form of reality, has a direct effect on their budget because they don't want to be responsible for it in the first place.

10. When does a homebuilder need an architect?

GC 1: For residential work, this is purely based on choice. There are a lot of GC's who are well equipped to handle your design ideas and offer their own ideas. They enjoy the creative involvement in your project. Often they will use CAD (computer aided drafting) to get you where you want to be.

GC 2: Often times the Architect and Interior Designer can work together to create a wonderful living space!

An Architect, if used, is useful with load bearings, size of rooms, open space decisions, flow of space, hard decisions that must be made to reduce the cost, or decisions that must be made to follow the chain of liability.

How to Hire an Interior Designer

An **Interior Designer** is helpful in many ways. He/She will help with space planning, the concept of color as it relates to how one chooses to live, flow of space, choosing a balance of quality interior finish against the budget, all floor coverings, and exterior color of building.

We believe working with an Interior Designer is a vital component of your building process. Your interior designer can make the difference between having a nice home to having an impressive home. Some of you are gifted with the skills of an interior designer and may not need to hire someone to help you. However, the majority of readers will benefit from the professional relationship with an interior designer

An interior designer will give you a new vision or expand your vision. He/she will encourage you to have a "wow" factor somewhere in your project. An interior designer will:

- Help you avoid buying mistakes by developing a Master Plan that will flow and be cohesive through the structure. Avoiding buying mistakes will save you money and disappointment.

- Know the design rules and how and when to

break them. This is especially important when you have or are after an eclectic look.

- Have experience and knowledge about where to shop. This is of value to you because it will save time.

- Ask you questions that will pull from you what constitutes the theme or look that is yours, not his/ or her style. This is important because your home needs to reflect the best of you.

- Help you decide how to use your budgeted funds wisely. He/she will mix price points so the line between great quality and lesser quality is blurred.

- Do the pre-shopping and "running" for you as part of developing the Master Plan. This is especially important to working wives and mothers.

- Often is a "tie-breaker" between a husband and wife. The decision he/she makes comes from professionalism, not a desire to pair up with either the husband or wife. An interior designer can be hired to stay with you throughout the whole project. That is worth a lot, knowing he/she will arrange your furniture as it comes in the door and correctly and artistically hang your pictures and place your accessories.

- Assist in picking your paint colors and schemes. He/she knows your fears around this part of the job and will hold your hand through this process. An interior designer is a good sounding board. Active listening by a designer is a skill that will support you in getting your best outcome.

- This will help you with your building or re-modeling project in ways even she/he can't explain. You could hear your designer say "This is right, I can't explain it, I just know."

- Be interested in a positive outcome since most of their business comes by word of mouth. He/she is committed to doing an excellent job because he is capable and because she would love a referral from you.

Questions to Ask an Interior Designer

1. Ask for references. Call at least three of them

2. Do you have a portfolio of your work?

3. Can I see your work up close and personal? Can I go look at your work?

4. How do you handle differences between parties involved in the building process?

5. Can you give me two examples of how you have mediated a conflict between spouses in regards to the interior design process?

6. Describe the steps you take to repair

incomplete or defective work of subcontractors you work with.

7. Describe your process, steps or methods of interior design when working with a client.

8. What is included in your interior design services? Ask for specifics.

9. Do you have a contract?

If you would like to hire Sandy as part of your professional team, visit our website at www.buildremodelforcouples.com

Here are a few questions that can help you find the right person. An interior designer can help from beginning to the end of your project or with small assignments.

What an Interior Designer Wants you to Know

- She is committed to making your house look like you and not her own.

- He understands that trust is earned, not a given.

- She desires to be a team player.

- He will have his favorite craftspeople that he will want you to use. He also understands he is under your employment. He can adjust to different craftspeople and different ways if you so desire.

- She will negotiate her fees.

- He may be paid a commission at some retail stores.

- She has the ability to buy at wholesale and sell at retail prices.

- He is charging you for the end result he intends to deliver.

How to Hire a Therapist or Life Coach

Some of you will be fortunate to live in an area where there is a team approach (interior designer and therapist/life coach combination) like Sandy and Laura. In most situations, Sandy includes a few coaching sessions in her contract. The client knows the coaching services are available to them when needed. Other times, Sandy invites Laura to be part of the process when she feels it would be helping her clients. If you would like to include Laura as a part of your team visit our website at www.buildremodelforcouples.com

We want you to have the best team to help your through your project, keep your eyes on your goals and love in your relationship!

Questions to Ask a Therapist or Life Coach

It's wise to put as much research into finding the right therapist or life coach to work with as you did in finding the perfect General Contractor and/or Builder. Today, with technology it is much easier to work with a therapist or life coach over the phone or on services such as Skype. In other words, the therapist or life coach doesn't necessarily need to live in your location. Here are a few questions to ask potential professionals.

1. Have you ever remodeled or built your home from ground up? If so, what were some of the challenges in your own relationship during their project? How did you deal with them?

2. What is your approach in working with couples?

3. Tell me about your experience in working with multiple team members? (Other therapists, family members, doctors,, interior designers, etc. You want to work with someone who has experience in facilitating groups of people)

4. Ask for references and call at least three of them.

5. What are your fees and do you have a contract?

What a Therapist or Life Coach Wants You to Know

An experienced, skilled and trusted Therapist or Life Coach is a vital member of your team. Here are a couple straightforward points to keep in mind:

• Don't wait until your relationship is really in trouble to bring a Therapist or Life Coach onto your team. Bring him or her onto the team early. You have an expert (painter, electrician, plumber, etc.) in every other area of your project. Why not have a relationship expert on hand?

- The strengths you bring to the project and your relationship build a strong foundation for your undertaking. Your weaknesses can erode that same foundation. Don't be surprised when things begin to crumble. Your relationship doesn't have to deteriorate or fall apart. Your therapist or life coach can help you through the rough times.

- The process of remodeling or building your home can be very rewarding. Remember to enjoy the process and one another.

A Therapist or Life Coach can help you keep your eyes and heart focused on your relationship throughout your remodel or building. This encouraging resource can be used as much or little as needed. You can benefit from including a Therapist or Life Coach if:

- You like to be prepared and have as many resources as possible to help you be successful.

- Your relationship has problem solving and communication challenges PRIOR to your home construction plans.

- You understand the benefits of nurturing, developing and preserving your relationship.

- You've been in therapy or worked with a Life Coach before.

- Your relationship gets stuck or unhealthy.

- You're concerned the stress will cause you major marriage problems.

Paperclip Electrical Design Tip 2: With all due respect to electricians, it will behoove you to watch them carefully. Yes, we know most of them are really cute, but we don't mean that kind of watch them! Watch where they place outlets and thermostats and all the other electrical gadgets you need. Be specific and thorough. Do you know how many times we have seen thermostats placed almost in the center of a wall where you may want to hang a picture? Way too many times.

Resources

Life Coaching/Therapist
- Laura Longville
  http://www.buildremodelforcouples.com
  - Life Coaching, Therapy, Intensives, Book, Workshops

Interior Designer
- **Sandy Berendes**
  http://www.buildremodelforcouples.com
  - Interior Design Services, Book, Workshops

Home Design
- *Take the U out of Clutter*, by Carmen Renee Berry and Mark Brunetz

- www.hunterdouglas.com.
  This is a beautiful website about window treatment fashion. You will experience the art of window dressing.

- www.pantone.com.
  This company has the standard language for color communication from designer to manufacturer

to retailer to customer. It is the world-renowned authority on color and provider of color systems.

- www.sherwinwilliams.com
  Sherwin-Williams Paints has partnered with Pottery Barn to offer their beautiful colors in the Sherwin-William paint stores. A great idea!

- www.kichler.com.
  This is a beautiful website with a lot of educational components, like Lighting 101.

- www.deltafaucets.com and www.kohler.com are two must see sites for kitchen and bathroom fixtures.

- www.shawfloors.com.
  This flooring website has a broad spectrum of the latest offerings by the flooring industry.

- http://www.howstuffworks.com.
  A website full of helpful information.

Financial Resources
- Olivian Mellan
  http://www.moneyharmony.com/index.html
  - Books, teleclasses and other resources

- Rick Kahler
  http://kahlerfinancial.com
  - Wealth Planning, Books and Seminars

- Dr.s Ted and Brad Klontz
  http://www.yourmentalwealth.com
  - Psychologists, Books, Financial Planning, Seminars and Consulting

- Crown Ministries
  http://www.crown.org
  - Christian Money Resources, Books, Radio, Seminars

Celebrate

B Y THE TIME YOU'VE GOTTEN TO THIS PART OF the book you have committed a lot of time, money, resources and energy to your home construction goals. If you answered the reflection questions you've discovered more about yourself, your spouse, your relationship, individual and relationship dreams, goals and values. You are amazing!

> *"It's all about the memories"*
> ~Laura Longville

Making a commitment to successfully prepare ahead of time for your remodel or home building adventure is admirable. You are exceptional and we trust that love will persevere in your relationship during the course of your project.

Because of your hard work, dedication and perseverance, a celebration is needed! In fact, why not celebrate throughout your whole project? Here are a few ideas to get you started.

- Have a groundbreaking ceremony with family and friends.

- Bring pizza, sub sandwiches or fried chicken and beer to your home site to celebrate the progress with family, friends and construction workers.

- Have family members inscribe their names or handprints on the foundation of your home.

- Write your favorite scripture and/or quotes on the stud walls of your home.

- Document the advancement of your project by taking pictures each week. You can create a photo album of your choosing.

- Keep family and friends updated on the details of your remodel or home building by blogging or tweeting about it.

- Have an open house inviting the laborers who worked with you. Invite suppliers who contributed products to your project. It is fun for the laborers and suppliers to see the finished project and celebrate your success with you!

- Soon after you have moved into your new home, have your church pastor, priest or rabbi come to the home for a blessing or ritual of celebration of your sacred space.

"Go confidently in the direction of your dreams. Live the life you have imagined."

~Henry David Thoreau

🔑 Create Your Own Key Ring

EACH KEY DESCRIBED IN THIS BOOK IS VITAL AND valuable. Each one opens the lock to the front door of your renovated or newly built home. If you've ever looked at an actual key, the kind with teeth, each one is unique. Keys can look alike, yet when you examine them closely each ridge, swoop or point are different. Your car or safety deposit key will not unlock the door to your home.

A key card, like the one you get at a hotel, stores a physical or digital signature that the door mechanism accepts before disengaging the lock. The signature to room 310 differs from that of room 103. On certain locks you'll need a combination, a sequence of number and/ or letters to open the door. Sometimes you'll find this on your car or garage door. You get the idea?

Here's a quick review of each Key that will open the door on your new home or remodel project. If you would like to keep all of the ideas and work you've done throughout each chapter in one section; transfer the information to this section for a "one stop" location.

KEY 1: Make Sure the Timing is Right

Reasons the time is right for us to build or remodel now.

- Family:

- Market:

- Evidence we are willing to grow in our relationship:

- We have the right tools and support to get the job done:

- We are prepared:

Why is this important to us?

KEY 2: Dream Big, Real Big

You've completed the Dream Big, Real Big process with your spouse and have a vision for your project.

 ## KEY 3: Let Your Needs and Values be Your Guide.

What are my: NEEDS   VALUES

What are
my spouse's: NEEDS   VALUES

KEY 4: Plan Sensibly

This Key helps you know your money beliefs and promotes a financial plan of integrity (budget) that you will follow.

Our important money beliefs are . . .

We have created a financial plan that will serve our needs, values and goals.

 KEY 5: Live in Financial Integrity

How do you plan to live in financial integrity?

KEY 6: Expect the Unexpected

Preparing for surprises or unanticipated changes can ease the pain of the unforeseen.

How are we prepared for the unexpected?

 ## KEY 7: Survive the Stress

This Key helps you identify when stress is running the project, what to do if you get stuck and learn easy communication tools to keep moving forward.

List three coping tools you are going to use when life gets stressful:

1.

2.

3.

Key Home Construction Team Contacts

NAMES OF OUR KEY TEAM PLAYERS	PHONE/TEXT NUMBERS	EMAIL
General Contractor		
Interior Designer		
Therapist or Life Coach		

You need each one of these keys for your construction project key ring. Every single key is required to secure a strong relationship while building or remodeling *your* home. It is advised to include each one of these keys on your key ring. You see, the teeth on the keys to your house are different from the teeth on the keys to Laura or Sandy's house. Sandy's house keys will not unlock the door of your home.

The teeth on each key, the physical or digital signature or combination, is the uniqueness of your relationship. Your dreams, goals, struggles, careers, family, friends or life events are specific to you. They make up the keys you put on your key ring.

The key ring is what holds all the keys together in one place. We want the key ring to represent the love in your relationship and celebration of the completion of your project. Your relationship, the love for one another (the key ring), and the keys will secure your home and keep the love in your relationship.

If you follow the advice in this book, you will have an easier time building or remodeling your house with your spouse and hopefully have fun!

"Give me the keys".
~Sam Shephard,
True West

We hope the instructions, the shared stories and the interior design tips will help you accomplish your home construction goals and keep the love in your relationship. We want your home construction to lead to a home full of love, respect and comfort. We wish you success!

We leave you with a prayer for your
home from Marianne Williamson:
May this house be a sacred dwelling
for those who live here.
May those who visit feel the peace
we have received from you.
May darkness not enter.
May the light of God shield this house from harm.
May the angels bring their peace here and
use our home as a haven of light.
May all grow strong in this place of healing, our
sanctuary from the loudness of the world.
May it so be used by You forever.
Amen

~Sandy and Laura

Appendix A

Dream Big, Real Big Process
Diagram 2

Dream Big, Real Big-Think and visualize about all you need, want and desire for your project

Your ideas here

Initial Reality Check-does this blueprint represent what we had in mind? Where do we need to make changes? Is there anything missing?

Your ideas here

Architect/Draftsman reworks the blueprint to reflect your changes.

There is an agreement between all parties that this is the plan to follow. There is a feeling of peace

Appendix B

Needs and Values Questionnaire

This questionnaire was originally designed to be used as a tool in life coaching. It was designed by Cheryl Weir and Associates and is in its original format. We believe this tool will help you identify your needs and values and how they influence and guide your home construction goals.

The *Needs and Values Questionnaire* begins with the attached assessment tool. Coaching is then structured around getting your needs met and orienting your life around your true values. You will begin to see how your unique needs and values give you your success while possibly limiting you. At the same time, you will become aware other people have different needs and values, providing new perspectives.

The *Needs and Values Program* assessment is not a test. Your score is not graded and comparisons are not made with other participants. According to current research on leadership, the most effective people are those who understand themselves, are aware of the demands of the situation, and then create strategies to meet those needs.

It will take approximately fifteen minutes to complete this assessment. Please find a quiet space with few distractions. Answer each question without spending a lot of time analyzing each question.

The *Needs and Values Program* will help you:

- Identify your top five needs
- Gain a better understanding about what drives you
- Determine the steps you might take in getting your needs met
- Identify your "true" values
- Begin to see that you are your values . . . what you are drawn to naturally
- Begin to see that living a values based life brings fulfillment
- Reach your goals more quickly!

PART I: NEEDS EVALUATION

Definitions: Needs are conditions, things, and feelings you *must* have to be minimally satisfied in life. Often, needs are the things that must be met before you can really "get on" with life. When you have unmet needs, you are usually "bound" or "hooked" by people, events and thoughts; you are more susceptible to being sad, depressed, angry or resentful. *Remember, needs are what you must have, not what you want, prefer or deserve.*

160

Wants, distinct from needs, are conditions, things or experiences you feel like you want to have to feel better about yourself, life, etc. Wants come from past experiences, upbringing, advertising or *unmet needs*. When your needs are met, you find that your want list has less of a pull on you. *Remember, Wants are what you want to have, but could actually live without.*

On a scale of 1 to 5, with one being 'more true' and 5 being 'less true,' rate the following:

SECTION 1

1 2 3 4 5 1. I need acceptance from most everyone.

1 2 3 4 5 2. I need acceptance from my family.

1 2 3 4 5 3. I need acceptance from a particular person.

1 2 3 4 5 4. I have a VERY hard time if I am not included in a conversation or event.

1 2 3 4 5 5. I have a VERY hard time if I don't perceive I am being accepted.

SECTION 2

1 2 3 4 5 1. I need to accomplish great things during my lifetime.

1 2 3 4 5 2. I need to accomplish something during my lifetime.

1 2 3 4 5 3. I need to almost always be engaged with accomplishing something.

1 2 3 4 5 4. I have a VERY hard time just relaxing or doing nothing special for several weeks.

1 2 3 4 5 5. I have a VERY hard time if I don't feel like I am accomplishing anything worthwhile.

SECTION 3

1 2 3 4 5 1. I need to be acknowledged by most everyone I help or work with.

1 2 3 4 5 2. I need to be acknowledged or complimented when I look good.

1 2 3 4 5 3. I need to be acknowledged by only one or just a few of my closest friends.

1 2 3 4 5 4. I have a VERY hard time if people don't sandwich a layer of criticism between two layers of praise.

1 2 3 4 5 5. I have a VERY hard time if I don't get acknowledged or complimented regularly.

SECTION 4

1 2 3 4 5 1. I need to be loved by many people.

1 2 3 4 5 2. I need to be loved by a close circle of friends.

1 2 3 4 5 3. I need to be loved by one particular person.

1 2 3 4 5 4. I have a VERY hard time if I don't believe an important person really loves me.

1 2 3 4 5 5. I have a VERY hard time if I don't feel loved enough.

SECTION 5

1 2 3 4 5 1. I need to be accurate or right in most situations.

1 2 3 4 5 2. I need to be accurate or right in my area of expertise.

1 2 3 4 5 3. I need to be accurate or right all or most of the time.

1 2 3 4 5 4. If I am mistaken about something, I take it personally.

1 2 3 4 5 5. If I make a mistake, I take it personally and hard.

SECTION 6

1 2 3 4 5 1. I need to be cared for/loved by many people.

1 2 3 4 5 2. I need to be cared for/loved by a select group of people.

1 2 3 4 5 3. I need to be cared for/loved by one particular person.

1 2 3 4 5 4. When I don't feel cared for, I get resentful and even bitter.

1 2 3 4 5 5. If I don't feel cared for, I have a VERY hard time.

SECTION 7

1 2 3 4 5 1. I need what people say to be perfectly clear.

1 2 3 4 5 2. I need to be certain about what I am working on, reading about or hearing about.

1 2 3 4 5 3. I need to be able to hear clearly what people are saying.

1 2 3 4 5 4. I have a VERY hard time if I am not clear about something important to me.

1 2 3 4 5 5. I have a VERY hard time if I am not certain about what is going on.

SECTION 8

1 2 3 4 5 1. I need a very comfortable bed in which to sleep.

1 2 3 4 5 2. I need the most comfortable job there is.

1 2 3 4 5 3. I need "all the comforts of home" when I travel.

1 2 3 4 5 4. If I know I may/will be uncomfortable in an otherwise interesting situation/place, I'll probably not go anyway.

1 2 3 4 5 5. When I am not comfortable, I am VERY grumpy or "put out."

SECTION 9

1 2 3 4 5 1. I need to say what's on my mind, even if it's not always appropriate.

1 2 3 4 5 2. I need others to say exactly what's on their mind, even if I won't like it or they don't want to.

1 2 3 4 5 3. I need only the key people in my life to communicate fully with me.

1 2 3 4 5 4. When I hold back and not fully tell someone what must be said, I start winding down and lose energy.

BREAK GROUND WITHOUT BREAKING UP

1 2 3 4 5 5. When others don't fully communicate with me, I get UPSET, concerned or frightened.

SECTION 10

1 2 3 4 5 1. I need the option to stop things if they don't go the way I want/need them to.

1 2 3 4 5 2. I need to keep the upper hand in most situations.

1 2 3 4 5 3. I need to tell people what to do.

1 2 3 4 5 4. If others start telling me what to do, I react strongly.

1 2 3 4 5 5. If we can't do it my way, I'll likely leave or find people who will.

SECTION 11

1 2 3 4 5 1. I need to be the primary one who makes something happen.

1 2 3 4 5 2. I need to be the "critical link" in bringing two people together.

1 2 3 4 5 3. I need to be the person who is known as someone who has the magic of getting projects completed on time.

1 2 3 4 5 4. If I don't feel needed, I am VERY uncomfortable.

1 2 3 4 5 5. If something good happens, I could have been a part of it yet wasn't a part of it, I feel left out.

SECTION 12

1 2 3 4 5 1. I need to do exactly what my duty is to my family and friends.

1 2 3 4 5 2. I need to do my duty to my job, clients or employer.

1 2 3 4 5 3. I need to do my duty to my country and/ or church.

1 2 3 4 5 4. If I can't do my duty, as I see it, I feel "held back" or suppressed.

1 2 3 4 5 5. If my duty is not clear, I am uncomfortable.

SECTION 13

1 2 3 4 5 1. I need to feel physically unrestrained and free.

1 2 3 4 5 2. 1 need for my time to be my own.

1 2 3 4 5 3. I need for my thoughts, actions and choices to be my own.

1 2 3 4 5 4. If I feel obligated or expected to do something (even if I don't mind it), I feel somewhat trapped and restricted.

1 2 3 4 5 5. If I don't have the sense that I am free from people, circumstances or concerns, I am definitely UNHAPPY.

SECTION 14

1 2 3 4 5 1. I need everyone around me to tell the truth and not mislead or try to cheat me.

1 2 3 4 5 2. I need my close friends to be honest with me and not "hold back."

1 2 3 4 5 3. I need to tell the truth all the time.

1 2 3 4 5 4. When someone lies to me and I find out, I get VERY upset.

1 2 3 4 5 5. When I have compromised my own integrity, I get VERY upset.

SECTION 15

1 2 3 4 5 1. I need things around me to be in their proper place or order.

1 2 3 4 5 2. I need/want to make my bed each day.

1 2 3 4 5 3. I need/want a specific plan of action so I know what I am doing.

1 2 3 4 5 4. When my things are out of place or messy, I don't like it at all.

1 2 3 4 5 5. When things are said or done illogically, I don't like it, usually.

SECTION 16

1 2 3 4 5 1. I need quiet in my workspace.

1 2 3 4 5 2. I need quiet at home.

1 2 3 4 5 3. I need to protect my sense of equilibrium and inner peace.

1 2 3 4 5 4. When I am around commotion and noise for more than an hour or two, I begin

to lose my sense of self or security.

1 2 3 4 5 5. When I lose my sense of self, I have to go to a quiet place to recover it.

SECTION 17

1 2 3 4 5 1. I need the ability and opportunity to get what I want in life, no matter what.

1 2 3 4 5 2. I need all the power I can get.

1 2 3 4 5 3. I need the opportunity to change the course of things.

1 2 3 4 5 4. When I feel powerless, it's extremely frustrating.

1 2 3 4 5 5. When I have no one around me to manage or impact, I feel like a fish out of water.

SECTION 18

1 2 3 4 5 1. I need to be recognized for what I've done.

1 2 3 4 5 2. I need to be noticed for how I look or act.

1 2 3 4 5 3. I need to be known for something special.

1 2 3 4 5 4. When people don't know that I did something great, I am strongly tempted to make sure they find out, one way or another.

1 2 3 4 5 5. Accomplishment without recognition is not fully rewarding.

SECTION 19

1 2 3 4 5 1. I need to feel safe from what is likely to happen.

1 2 3 4 5 2. I need to feel safe from what might, yet is unlikely, to happen.

1 2 3 4 5 3. I need to make sure people that I am close to are fully protected from circumstances.

1 2 3 4 5 4. When I start something new and I'm not sure which dangers to protect myself from, I am uncomfortable.

1 2 3 4 5 5. When I don't take every possible precaution, I am uncomfortable.

SECTION 20

1 2 3 4 5 1. I need to perform a job or engage in regular work.

1 2 3 4 5 2. I need to keep busy with things.

1 2 3 4 5 3. I need to do even more than I am doing now.

1 2 3 4 5 4. When I am idle, I am nervous or uncomfortable.

1 2 3 4 5 5. When I am not working, I feel guilty.

PART 2: NEEDS SUMMARY

Summarize the Needs Evaluation on this summary form. First write the total score received for each Section (1-20) in the 'RANK' column. Next, circle the 5 lowest scores. These are your most critical needs

RANK NEED

_____ Section 1: Acceptance

_____ Section 2: Accomplishment

_____ Section 3: Acknowledgments/Compliments

_____ Section 4: Be Loved

_____ Section 5: Be Right

_____ Section 6: Cared For

_____ Section 7: Certainty/Clarity/Accuracy

_____ Section 8: Comfort

_____ Section 9: Communication (Pull)

_____ Section 10: Control/Dominate

_____ Section 11: Critical Link/Be Needed

_____ Section 12: Duty/Obligation

_____ Section 13: Freedom

_____ Section 14: Honesty/integrity

_____ Section 15: Order/Perfection

_____ Section 16: Peace/Quietness

_____ Section 17: Power

_____ Section 18: Recognition

_____ Section 19: Safety/Security

_____ Section 20: Work

PART 3: NEEDS INDEX

Circle the word that best describes the 'Exact Need' for each 'Area of Need.'

AREA OF NEED EXACT NEED

1. **Accepted**
   Approved
   Be Included
   Be Permitted
   Respected

2. **Accomplish**
   Achieve
   Fulfill
   Realize
   Finish

3. **Acknowledged**
   Complimented
   Appreciated
   Admired
   Valued

4. **Be Loved**
   Liked
   Cherished
   Esteemed
   Held Fondly

5. **Be Needed**
   Important
   Critical Link
   Useful
   Be Material

6. **Duty**
   Have a Task
   Do Right/Good
   Follow
   Obligated

7. **Freedom**
   Unrestricted
   Independent
   Privileged
   Immune

8. **Honesty**
   Uprightness
   Openness
   Frankness
   Integrity

9. **Be Right**
   Moral
   Correct
   Not Mistaken
   True

10. **Be Cared For**
    Attention
    Concerned
    Helpful
    Cared About

11. **Certainty**
    Clarity
    Accuracy
    Assurance
    Obviousness

12. **Comfort**
    Luxury
    Ease
    Contented
    Leisure

13. **Communicate**
    Be Heard
    Speak
    Share
    Inform

14. **Order**
    Perfection
    Placement
    Harmony
    Right-ness

15. **Peace**
    Quietness
    Stillness
    Serenity
    Balance

16. **Power**
    Authority
    Capacity
    Omnipotence
    Vigor

17. **Recognition**
    Be Noticed
    Remembered
    Known For
    Regarded Well

18. **Safety**
    Secure
    Protected
    Stable
    Known

19. **Control**
    Dominate
    Command
    Restrain
    Manage

20. **Work**
    Perform
    Labor
    Industrious
    Busy

PART 4: VALUES EVALUATION

Definitions: Values are who you are. That is, once your basic needs are met, you tend to want to express your values. Values are *not* needs. If you need something, it is not a value, even though it may appear to be essential. Once you experience your needs being satisfied and met, you see this distinction more clearly. *Remember, values are what you do or how you express yourself, after your needs are met.*

On a scale of 1 to 5, with one being 'more true' and 5 being 'less true,' how would you rate the following:

SECTION 1

1 2 3 4 5 1. I like activities like river rafting because you never now what's really around the bend.

1 2 3 4 5 2. I'd really love to pack up and take a month-long trip to Europe (or any place abroad); I'd leave next week!

1 2 3 4 5 3. If I had to choose between two ways of getting something done—the exciting, yet

unpredictable and possibly longer way or the most efficient way—I'd tend to take the more exciting way.

1 2 3 4 5 4. Sure, I could use a plan or map—but what fun is that, really?

1 2 3 4 5 5. There is nothing more important to me personally than being a part of an adventure.

SECTION 2

1 2 3 4 5 1. There is probably art in everything, but only certain things are worth looking at.

1 2 3 4 5 2. I tend to make whatever I touch more aesthetically pleasing.

1 2 3 4 5 3. Nature is the source of beauty.

1 2 3 4 5 4. If it's not beautiful, I probably won't like it.

1 2 3 4 5 5. There is nothing more important to me than seeing or experiencing the beauty of things, life, etc.

SECTION 3

1 2 3 4 5 1. After people meet, see or speak with me, they tend to get "into action" about something.

1 2 3 4 5 2. I like being the spark that gets people going again.

1 2 3 4 5 3. It turns me on when I see people turned on because of something I've said or done.

1 2 3 4 5 4. I tend to let people know how they can get the job done more easily and more productively.

1 2 3 4 5 5. There is nothing more important to me personally than being a catalyst or lever for change or movement.

SECTION 4

1 2 3 4 5 1. When someone asks me for directions, I usually take them a part of the way or draw a map so I am certain they won't get lost.

1 2 3 4 5 2. I tend to put other people's needs and concerns ahead of or equal to my own.

1 2 3 4 5 3. If I couldn't assist people or make some definite and powerful contributions, I'd begin to question what life is all about.

1 2 3 4 5 4. I get upset when I see people not being served or assisted when they easily could be.

1 2 3 4 5 5. There is nothing more important to me than serving people or humanity.

SECTION 5

1 2 3 4 5 1. The act of inventing or making up new things, ideas, art, form or function is very appealing and energizing to me.

1 2 3 4 5 2. I like to make things.

1 2 3 4 5 3. I get no personal reward from just watching or repeating someone else's ideas; they have to come from or be measurably customized by me.

1 2 3 4 5 4. I don't get bored; I find something creative to do or get involved with.

1 2 3 4 5 5. There is nothing more important to me personally than creating something that didn't really exist before I got involved.

SECTION 6

1 2 3 4 5 1. I would have really liked to have been a Christopher Columbus-type person, discovering something that has not been discovered.

1 2 3 4 5 2. I like finding the wrinkle in just about anything.

1 2 3 4 5 3. I love finding out new things about me and others.

1 2 3 4 5 4. Once I've found "it," I go looking for another "it."

1 2 3 4 5 5. There is nothing more important to me than discovering new things or new ways with things.

SECTION 7

1 2 3 4 5 1. It's important to me to express my feelings, even when it gets in the way of things.

1 2 3 4 5 2. I am grateful I can really experience the full range of emotions.

1 2 3 4 5 3. I am glad I can cry.

1 2 3 4 5 4. I am able to laugh a lot.

1 2 3 4 5 5. There is nothing more important to me than experiencing my feelings and emotions.

SECTION 8

1 2 3 4 5 1. It's important someone step forward and take charge.

1 2 3 4 5 2. I tend to like to "rally the troops," to get people moving forward together.

1 2 3 4 5 3. I like to be called on to lead a team of people.

1 2 3 4 5 4. When I lead, I don't put up with anything from anybody.

1 2 3 4 5 5. There is nothing more important to me than leading people.

SECTION 9

1 2 3 4 5 1. I feel compelled to be the best that I can be.

1 2 3 4 5 2. I tend to be the most able and qualified person I know of in my area or field – and I feel good about that.

1 2 3 4 5 3. I'd strongly prefer to be a master of a trade than a "jack of all trades".

1 2 3 4 5 4. I would be fully willing to be completely ignorant in several important areas if it meant that I could be a master of one.

1 2 3 4 5 5. Nothing is more important to me than to be master or the master of my trade.

SECTION 10

1 2 3 4 5 1. A strong and consistent theme throughout my life has been my quest of personal and physical pleasure.

1 2 3 4 5 2. I can never "feel good" enough.

1 2 3 4 5 3. Without a lot of pleasure, what's the use of living.

1 2 3 4 5 4. If it feels good, I do it.

1 2 3 4 5 5. There is nothing more important to me than experiencing as many forms of pleasure as possible.

SECTION 11

1 2 3 4 5 1 I get high from being included in other's lives or plans.

1 2 3 4 5 2. If the phone doesn't ring or I don't get letters from friends, I tend to wind down or get depressed.

1 2 3 4 5 3. We are so lucky there are 6 billion people on this planet! (More people to love!)

1 2 3 4 5 4. The bond between two people is God's greatest gift to us.

1 2 3 4 5 5. There is nothing more important to me personally than to be very connected with people.

SECTION 12

1 2 3 4 5 1. I will shop at a store with higher prices but only with clerks who are really nice and helpful.

1 2 3 4 5 2. It is better to be polite than to get what you really want in a situation.

1 2 3 4 5 3. I am upset when people are not polite or nice to me on the phone or in person.

1 2 3 4 5 4. I am so sensitive that I can't be around people who are upset, needy or loud. I protect my "space."

1 2 3 4 5 5. There is nothing more important to me personally than being sensitive and/or nice, or being around those who are.

SECTION 13

1 2 3 4 5 1. I have a strong relationship with God or the "universal being."

1 2 3 4 5 2. I have surrendered my life to God's will for me.

1 2 3 4 5 3. I get tremendous pleasure and strength from praying, meditating or being with God.

1 2 3 4 5 4. If there wasn't really a God, I would create one for myself.

1 2 3 4 5 5. There is nothing more important to me personally than being in constant touch with God.

SECTION 14

1 2 3 4 5 1. I enjoy passing on information and ideas to the next generation.

1 2 3 4 5 2. When I teach others, I get tremendous satisfaction.

1 2 3 4 5 3. It almost doesn't matter what the subject matter is, I just love to teach.

1 2 3 4 5 4. I get pleasure from teaching, even to a class of one.

1 2 3 4 5 5. There is nothing more important to me than to teach.

SECTION 15

1 2 3 4 5 1. I tend to justify the means to get to an end I really want.

1 2 3 4 5 2. Many people are just born to lose.

1 2 3 4 5 3. I compete well with a group or against myself.

1 2 3 4 5 4. I get a tremendous high from pulling something off or winning.

1 2 3 4 5 5. There is nothing more important to me than winning at something.

PART 5: VALUES SUMMARY

Summarize the Values Evaluation on this summary form. First write the total score received for each Section (1-15) in the 'RANK' column. Next, circle the 5 lowest scores. These are your most "true" Values.

RANK VALUE

_____ Section 1: Adventure

_____ Section 2: Beauty

_____ Section 3: Catalyst

_____ Section 4: Contributions/Service

_____ Section 5: Creativity

_____ Section 6: Discovery/Learning

_____ Section 7: Emotions/Feelings

_____ Section 8: Leadership

_____ Section 9: Mastery

_____ Section 10: Pleasure

_____ Section 11: Relatedness

_____ Section 12: Sensitivity/Niceness

_____ Section 13: Spirituality/God

_____ Section 14: Teaching

_____ Section 15: Winning

PART 6: VALUES INDEX
Circle the word that best describes the 'Exact Value' for each 'Area of Value.'

AREA OF VALUE EXACT VALUE

1. **Adventure**
   The Unknown
   Thrill
   Danger/Dare
   Risk

2. **Beauty**
   Appreciation
   Grace
   Refinement
   Magnificence

3. **Catalyst**
   Impact/Move
   Touch/Turn On
   Unstuck-er
   Coach

4. **Mastery**
   The Best
   Proficiency
   Expert
   Excellence

5. **Pleasure**
   Indulgence
   Gratification
   Sensuality
   Hedonism

6. **Relatedness**
   Networker
   Connected
   Linked/Allied
   Be Structure

7. **Contribute**
    Serve
    Improve
    Augment
    Assist

8. **Creativity**
    Be Source
    Design
    Invent
    Synthesize

9. **Discovery**
    Learn
    Detect
    Locate
    Realize

10. **Feelings**
    Emotions
    Drama
    Sentiment
    Empathy

8. **Leadership**
    Influence
    Manage
    Guide
    Motivate

11. **Sensitivity**
    Gracious
    Pleasant
    Inviting
    Tender

12. **Spirituality**
    God
    Faith/Trust
    Eternity
    Religion

13. **Teaching**
    Instruct
    Educate
    Train
    Illuminate

14. **Winning**
    Take/Get/Own
    Compete
    Engage
    Victory

About the Authors

Sandy Berendes is a professional Interior Designer who was licensed and registered by the Texas Board of Architectural Examiners in 1993. She has enjoyed membership in several professional Interior Design and Civic Organizations. She grows in her career as a designer by continuing to update her skills through attending seminars and markets, and studying and reading books by other designers.

Through the last twenty years, she has passionately worked with two hundred plus clients who are updating, remodeling or building homes. She has also built two homes of her own and recognizes this is a stressful time for couples. Her "take away" after completing her design assignments for a job is a great sense of fulfillment and satisfaction. Seeing her clients' love of her work continues to be a reward like none other.

The cloud in all this has been and still is has been witnessing the stress or struggle between couples during their home projects. Couples often have said building was hard on their relationship, but they are glad they did it. Hence this book has come to pass.

Sandy lives in her hometown of Rapid City, SD in a vintage 1946 cottage home with a white picket fence in the yard and two not-so-darling cats. She is the mother of two successful and productive children, five princesses who are also her adored granddaughters, and one little handsome prince of a grandson.

Laura Longville and her husband, Mark, of 28 years built their dream home together in 2011 with the help of Sandy Berendes. Building their home together was stressful and amazing at the same time. Launching their dream came on the heels of major change in their lives. After 3 significant deaths in their family, they decided to move ahead with designing and creating the home they had been envisioning for over 25 years. Their personal experience in building their home is the foundation for Laura's enthusiasm for the book.

For well over 28 years Laura has worked as a counselor, trainer, speaker and life coach. She founded and is CEO of Walking in Grace, Inc.; a faith based counseling and life coaching center in Rapid City, SD. Laura is also a consulting therapist for Onsite Workshops in Nashville, TN the national leader in therapeutic programs. She has always found innovative and creative approaches to equip people to know themselves deeply and find hope and healing.

Please visit www.buildremodelforcouples.com to contact Sandy or Laura.

CPSIA information can be obtained at www.ICGtesting.com
Printed in the USA
LVOW05s0039150115

422480LV00005B/6/P